entrecode®

Unlocking the entrepreneurial DNA

entrecode®

Unlocking the entrepreneurial DNA

David Hall

How to start, grow and revitalise your business

First published in 2013 by Management Books 200 Ltd
36 Western Road
Oxford OX1 4LG
Tel: 0044 (0) 1865 600738
Email: info@mb2000.com
Web: www.mb2000.com

British Library Cataloguing in Publication Data is available

ISBN 9781852526986

Acknowledgements

My sincere thanks to Andy Forrester who helped me write this book. His help and advice throughout has been invaluable.

A huge thank you to Jagadish Shenoy who helped me to research the immensely inspiring story of Veena Patil in Chapter Eight.

A very special thank you to Lynn Bradshaw, my Personal Assistant, who has worked long hours typing and reworking the manuscript whilst also managing to keep me on the straight and narrow.

I could not have cracked the code without the help of Wyatt Woodsmall who helped me find the combination to the lock.

And finally, thank you to the entrepreneurs who are the stars of this book for sharing their stories and wisdom for the benefit of others.

Contents

Foreword

Foreword by Tim Atterton, Managing Director – Business Dynamics, Perth W.A.

E**ntrepreneurs work in mysterious** ways; this is the conclusion David Hall has come to after years of working with some of the finest wealth and job creators.

After years of research and observations, Hall has broken down the cocoon of mystery that surrounds their inner thoughts and so opened the way to a better understanding of their drivers and ways that they see the world differently from the rest of us.

Up to now it has been easier to say what they are not rather than what they are.

They are neither Del Boy-type spivs, nor get-rich-quick merchants out to make a quick buck.

They don't dress to impress nor do they madly socialize with their fellow human beings.

They don't aggressively make money only to retreat to some Caribbean island and bury it in the sand. Interestingly, there is much evidence to support the view that they are keener to contribute to society than take.

Now Hall, with 30 years' experience in helping entrepreneurs attain their goals, has broken into the inner mind of these extraordinary men and women.

In this book you will find the personal stories of many entrepreneurs and meet the extraordinary Wyatt Woodsmall, the American scientist who has trained Olympic athletes to tap into their intuitive mental strengths and go on to triumph. On meeting Woodsmall, Hall recognized that together they could open the mysterious gate that gives access to the world of the entrepreneurial mind but only to those in possession of the code.

Until this code was cracked we could never gain access to the inner mind of the entrepreneur.

More importantly, without the code being cracked it was impossible to pass on the secrets of the entrepreneur to people everywhere keen to give starting, growing or revitalising a business their best shot.

This book describes how the code was eventually cracked and introduces the reader to entrepreneurs who have moved from the darkness into light. In effect this book describes the DNA of entrepreneurial success. The timing could not be better, as the Western world languishes in the shadow of the longest recession it has ever experienced. New jobs must be created to replace the old. Now is the time to do it.

I have known David Hall for more than thirty years and have watched his journey into the hearts and minds of entrepreneurs with fascination. His observations challenge many existing conventions; but will resonate strongly with both entrepreneurs and those that work with them on a daily basis. The insights in this book are rare and unique; and will help us to understand the psyche of the entrepreneur before we seek to change them. Most of all, I hope that this book goes some way to convincing readers from a professional management background that we need to be more like entrepreneurs, rather than deriding their management approach and encouraging them to be more like us!

This is a book that demands to be read.

Chapter One
The Challenge
Facing the World

Most thinking people can recall a Eureka moment when they found a solution to some long-standing problem that had been keeping them awake at night. This book owes its birth to just such a moment in my life. I had been struggling for years to try to solve a mystery. How do entrepreneurs start, grow and revitalise businesses successfully? If we knew the secret of their success we could help many more to thrive and grow and create the wealth and jobs desperately needed in most countries which are struggling today.

As someone who had made a life-time career out of studying and advising companies, it was a question that bothered me when I published my book *In the Company of Heroes* in 1999. But it bothers me much more now in the wake of the global economic crisis and the onset of the worst recession since the 1930s.

Most governments around the world have pinned their hopes on a self-correcting recovery. Cut back on government spending and the market will itself come up with the new jobs we need. I really hope it works out, but in the meantime unemployment has soared – particularly youth unemployment – and society has been paying the cost in terms of social unrest and rioting.

So could there be an alternative? I am not thinking of a model in which the state picks winners and pumps in subsidy to encourage them to grow – that's been tried before and it ended in dismal failure. No, my suggestion, based on 30 years of working with new companies, is to tap into the hidden resources of entrepreneurial spirit and let it work its magic.

Hold on, I hear you say. That sounds just what the British government has been advocating, twisting the arms of the banks to pump money into the small businesses in the hope of seeing the miracle begin.

Believe me, that won't work. For pumping money into ill-prepared small business will achieve virtually nothing. In my experience, what new businesses require if they're to succeed is not a soft bank loan but an ability to spot a good business idea (what I call a *superior opportunity*) based on solving their customers' problems. You will find plenty of examples in this book of what I mean.

But superior opportunities are not in themselves enough. Businesses that want to grow also need leadership and vision. That comes invariably from the entrepreneur. Without this key resource small companies can never become serious employers. At the moment there's a log jam in precisely this part of the 'growing a business' model. To make the point you only need look at the latest figures on small business. In Europe, for example, there are at present approximately 20 million small businesses. Sounds impressive, but 90 percent of them employ 10 or fewer people. The vast majority stay small until their owners put them quietly to bed.

If we are to have an expanding economy based on companies with the capacity for continual growth – you'll find examples of such companies in this book – there is a pressing need to find the entrepreneurs with the skills to guide the new businesses through those rough early years.

If we can release the log jam and get the businesses flowing strongly in the right direction the sky is the limit because our research suggests that as many as 15 percent of the population have the necessary aptitude and skills, while only 2 per cent ever make use of them. This is a waste of talent, both for the individuals and society as a whole.

So how can we increase the supply of entrepreneurs?

I believe it requires two steps. The first is to unlock the 'skills locker' of the successful entrepreneurs, skills that are often kept hidden in the mind of the founding entrepreneur, safely guarded by a coded lock. We need to crack this code if we are ever to achieve expansion.

The second step is to train people how to be entrepreneurs. It's often argued that entrepreneurs are born not bred. But my research and my experience of working with would-be entrepreneurs has proved this not to be the case. I have shown, using my methods, that entrepreneurial behaviour and skills can be successfully developed. There is no reason why entrepreneurial colleges could not be established in Britain, elsewhere in Europe and even around the world – following the approaches I have devised in collaboration with existing entrepreneurs. This is the first spin-off from my successful cracking of the entrepreneurial code.

In Britain, very little useful research has been conducted with regard to the entrepreneurial mind. Until recently all we could say was that while no two entrepreneurs were alike, they shared certain distinct traits. Again, you will understand when you read the varied accounts of our selected entrepreneurs.

Entrepreneurs tend to be obsessive and highly focused people. They are hard-wired to spot business opportunities that others overlook. While they often become very rich, it is not a love of money that motivates them but the challenge of bringing a product or a service successfully to the marketplace. Most important of all is the vision and the charisma they bring to bear on the job in hand, inspiring loyalty and trust with the people they work with.

But years of being involved with entrepreneurs has taught me something else. They are not very good at explaining to others just why they have made a decision one way rather than another. Driven forward by a vision, a compelling vision, they often find it difficult to convey exactly how they go about turning this vision into reality. At times they seem to be deliberately holding back critical information from people who really ought to be in the loop.

I have observed this inexplicable shortcoming for ten years or more. To me it appeared there was a barrier between the entrepreneur and lesser mortals – one that could be crossed only by people who had access to the secret code. I came to think that only cracking the code would allow me to understand what went on in the mind of the entrepreneur. But how could it be cracked?

I wrestled with this dilemma for several years until I met an American expert in the developing science of working with high-performing people. This was Wyatt Woodsmall, a man famous as the coach of the US High Diving Team in successive Olympic Games. His speciality was to break down the human psyche, teach athletes how to get themselves ready for action by moving into 'The Zone' and establishing a winning mindset. He coached the team, whose most celebrated hero was Greg Louganis. In two Olympics he brought home a haul of four Olympic Golds. Wyatt's skills of coaching people to maximise their talents are legendary. He was recruited to coach the American military elite on how to improve their performance in various fields.

When I met Wyatt in his home in Washington DC, he and I got along famously. He assured me he could devise a programme that would help us to understand the performance of entrepreneurs. He could train them to think in new ways, he would make them world beaters.

I flew him over from Washington DC to work in tandem with me and a group of volunteer entrepreneurs from Yorkshire. Once he had conducted his analysis, he could add new observations that altered entirely my understanding of how entrepreneurs think.

He told us that they were, almost without exception, people who had had very negative experiences in childhood or adolescence, but the bad experiences were often tempered by a good one. (I thought at the time *"That's me."*) However, it was his final revelation that really struck home. Entrepreneurs, he concluded, were creative and innovative people, whereas many human beings are procedural and process oriented.

What did that mean exactly? He explained that procedural people were by nature logical, analytical, and fond of engaging in long discussions. Innovators, on the other hand, were good at synthesis, creativity and intuitive thinking, but had a very short attention span. The distinction made a huge contribution to my views on how to get the best out of entrepreneurs. The artificial barrier between me and the entrepreneurs began to be broken down. The code was beginning to be cracked.

In short, it is enough to say that we now understand much better how entrepreneurs start, grow and revitalise successful businesses. We can

identify those with natural talent using a newly devised test, and help those less gifted to significantly improve their performance and that of their business.

This effort to show how people with the right traits could be identified and developed has not yet become the norm in countries where entrepreneurs are in short supply – including not just the whole of Europe but the rest of the world. Am I fantasising when I imagine that the processes described in this book could form the basis of a new industrial revolution, one with a kinder and more inclusive face?

I defined entrepreneurship in my book *In the Company of Heroes* as **'people who create value often from practically nothing'**. Value creation can come from starting a business, growing it or even revitalising it. Value can also be created in large companies and public sector bodies by innovating and doing things more efficiently and effectively. It can also come from identifying and developing high performing people within organisations.

You will meet people in this book who have been entrepreneurial in all four situations. They clearly show that the **entrecode**® can add value at any stage in a business' life and, as I will demonstrate, in any national context. Over the past 20 years I have researched and worked with over 500 entrepreneurs around the world. They helped me crack the entrepreneurial code. In this book you will meet a representative sample. But these are not 'case studies' as presented in most business books. They are real life human stories of sheer guts, passion and determination. Stand back and be amazed. Let's meet them.

Hugh Facey – Gripple
Yorkshire wire man, Hugh Facey, has brought new life to Sheffield's steel industry. He seized a chance to rebuild the once-famous steel city, or part of it at least. He spotted an opportunity to create jobs by solving the problem sheep farmers had in repairing broken barbed wire fences – you can imagine how tricky that can be. He then expanded the market for his special 'Gripple' tool by teaming up with a big Australian fencing company to repair a fence over 1,000 miles long, a fence that allows Australian sheep farmers to sleep at night – the famous 'Dingo Fence'.

He now employs 350 people, and his business continues to grow across 5 continents. Meet Hugh in Chapter Two where he describes how he started his business after typically serving an apprenticeship at somebody else's expense. Hugh makes an appearance again in Chapter Thirteen where he describes how he has continued to innovate over 20 years.

Ann Adlington – Triple A Ranch

Who would have guessed that a trip to a dog kennel with her husband would lead Ann Adlington at the age of 45 to create a holiday resort for dogs and cats? Once she had the idea, she researched it thoroughly in the USA before opening her luxury dog's home and cattery, where animals received one-to-one attention, kept fit in an animal swimming pool (the cats usually turned it down) and generally had the life of Riley.

The project went off the rails when Mars (of Mars Bar fame) bought a majority share. Things became difficult but Ann has successfully moved into Carp Fishery, a wiser woman (warning: cats please keep out). Anne makes an appearance in Chapter Four where she describes how she revolutionised dog care.

Roger McKechnie – Derwent Valley Foods

Roger McKechnie is the man who brought adult snack foods to the UK. Back in the late 80s crisps and snacks were aimed at children. Roger spotted the opportunity to create adult snack foods and the Phileas Fogg brand was born, allowing adults to entertain at home with such delights as Mignons Morceaux. In Chapter Four Roger tells us how he created a whole new industry of adult snack foods.

The late John Noble and Andy Lane – Loch Fyne Oysters

John was a country gentlemen, Andy a man who camped in a rickety caravan on the beach. Their success is a perfect example of how the two men with no previous experience could found a company and turn it into a money-spinner. In less than five years they built up a world-renowned oyster and seafood company and brought jobs to the beautiful but isolated Loch Fyne community. John and Andy share their experiences in Chapter Five.

Tom Hunter – Sports Division

Tom featured in one of my earlier books and has gone on to much greater things since then. Tom started and grew a chain of sports shops which he eventually sold for £250 million. He then invested in numerous other businesses and became a billionaire. Tom was knighted in 2005 for his services to entrepreneurship and he is an entrepreneurial role model and a personal hero of mine. You will find out more about Tom in Chapter Five.

Jonathan Elvidge – The Gadget Shop

Jonathan saw that there was a gap in the market for a store where customers could pick up all they needed in the way of gadgetry in the one location. He soon had a chain of stores trading successfully all across Britain. But when the bank pulled his overdraft without warning he brought in venture capitalists to help expand the business and lost control of it. The business failed. Five years on, he bounced back to run Red5. Jonathan tells his story, warts and all, in Chapter Six.

Mike Firth – Yorkshire Foods

Mike Firth at 65 is the energetic organiser of the Yorkshire Business Convention, rubbing shoulders with the likes of Bill Clinton and Elle Macpherson. His speciality was the import and export of dried fruit, building his business up to be a major player on the American scene but he was harried out of California by threats and dirty tricks. He bounced right back in his native Yorkshire; he tells us how also in Chapter Eight.

Paul Cave – Sydney, Australia – BridgeClimb

Paul saw a perfect business opportunity to turn a famous tourist attraction into an unforgettable adventure. But he faced every conceivable obstacle on the way to achieving his objective. Persistence was the key to his ultimate success. Paul describes his amazing tale of persistence in Chapter Nine.

Veena Patil – Kesari Tours

Veena is an Indian Woman who runs a quite amazing worldwide travel business – for the new Indian middle-class. Her arrangements for *women*

only cruises and trips is a shrewd business response to give young women, whose husbands are too busy to take holidays a chance to see the world in the company of other women. Veena tells us how she grew her business into an international award-winning group in Chapter Ten.

Paul Mackie – Rex Procter & Partners
Paul Mackie took on the challenge of revitalising a business that was pretty set in its ways, flatlining in sales and profits. He applied himself to the task with great energy and provided the leadership, using my entrepreneurial principles to transform his business. Paul shares his amazing leadership adventure in Chapter Eleven.

Terry Bramall – Keepmoat
Terry Bramall took over the family building contractors from his father and developed it from a £25 million business that was losing money to the market leader in its sector. Keepmoat is a great example that illustrates the benefits of using my new principles to grow successfully. Terry sold his business to HBOS for £783 million in 2007. We meet Terry in Chapter Twelve.

Ajaz Ahmed – Freeserve
Beat this for a story! Ajaz Ahmed had spent 15 years running a Dixons store in Leeds. In 1999 the computer manufacturers and the Internet Service Providers launched new ranges of computers designed to work with broadband, instead of the irritating dial-up modem connections. Ajaz, who moved to Huddersfield with his family when he was three, bought a computer only to find getting online was not easy. Bloody slow in fact. Something of an electronics fiend, he worked out a plug-in system to make the job easier and went on to introduce a free service across the Internet paid for by advertising. It revolutionised life for millions of users. Five years later the business was sold to French Telecom for £1.9 billion pounds. Ajaz has launched his latest entrepreneurial venture, an online legal service that will produce another great leap forward. Meet Ajaz in Chapter Thirteen.

Dr Fiona Wood – Avita Medical

Fiona is an all-time Australian heroine who in 2005 received the Australian of the year award for her work with burns victims from the Bali bombing.

Fiona pioneered the new technology of 'spray-on skin' to dramatically improve the recovery of burns victims. She turned her innovation into a business which now sells world-wide.

Fiona uses the funds she receives from the business to invest in further research in order to develop her work. Read Fiona's remarkable story in Chapter Fourteen.

These are some of my heroes that helped me unlock the mystery of the **entrecode**®. This book is not based on academic theory but the sweat and toil of those who have been there and done it. It finally puts the pieces of the entrepreneurial jigsaw together. Are you ready to discover the magic of the code so you can join my successful band of heroes?

Unravelling the unwritten rules that govern how an entrepreneur will act in any situation is the major aim of this book.

Chapter Two
A Gripping Tale: Starting a Business

Once upon a time a sheep farmer was struggling with a barbed wire fence on the Welsh uplands. The ravages of time, and the pressure of an insistent flock, had brought the fence down at the corner of the field. Repairing it was a gruesome business. Wearing a pair of thick leather gloves and armed with a stout pair of pliers, the farmer slowly dragged the broken ends together, twisting the strands to make the fence secure, never a pleasant job but even less so in a persistent drizzle. Despite the gloves, it was not possible to avoid some tearing of battle hardened hands.

Out of circumstances like these emerged the idea of the Gripple. For just as the farmer's frustrations hit boiling point, so the story goes, a visitor called Hugh Facey came up on the scene. Hugh was the owner of a wire making company and a budding entrepreneur. He had come to sell wire but was to leave with the germ of a good business idea.

He found the farmer struggling with the broken barbed wire fence in the rain and it immediately became the subject of conversation. "Good afternoon, Hugh," said the farmer, taking off his gloves and revealing the damage to his hands, "if you could find some way to make this job easier, you'd be onto a winner. Thousands of farmers would come knocking on your door."

That evening, as Hugh drove back to his base in Sheffield, he turned the problem over in his mind and came up with a way forward. Why not have a joining device that could hold the wires together while the operator tightened them up in an easy manner. Eventually he coined a

name for it – 'The Gripple' – because it would both grip the wires and pull them together.

Once the Gripple was launched on the market some three years later Hugh never looked back, selling millions of these small gripping devices to grateful farmers across the country and across the world. In no time at all he had created a hundreds of jobs where only a few were employed before. That's the story, and it contains a kernel of truth. But before you learn what actually happened, let me tell you something of the remarkable Hugh, an entrepreneur's entrepreneur.

Although he looks every inch a no-nonsense Yorkshireman, stocky and with a ruddy face, Hugh's father was a Canadian vicar. His wife, Hugh's mother, came from the South East of England. "She was the original Essex girl," Hugh jokes, "that's why we're a bit crackers."

Being a little crackers is certainly a quality that is found in many successful entrepreneurs, for entrepreneurs do not think and behave as ordinary mortals do, as we'll see in the course of this book. They are also; on the whole, people who have failed to blossom at school, finding the academic bias in most educational systems not to their taste. Most can't see the point of abstract learning. In the course of my 30 years of working with them I have seen this time and time again. While Hugh found his secondary school tedious and uninspiring, he showed early signs of having a good business brain: "I was always entrepreneurial," he told me, "my sister used to say we all got half-a-crown, but I always had five bob at the end of the week and she had nothing." This may in part be down to the fact he had a milk-round to deliver at the early age of eight.

Hugh grew up to love Sheffield, a town he has called home for over 50 years. He was fascinated by the steel industry. It was in this city that the secrets of stainless steel had been discovered in 1914, making the city the cutlery capital of the world. So when he left school he gravitated towards a job in the steel business, taking an engineering qualification at the Colne Valley Technical College.

On graduating at the age of 21 he was taken on as a trainee at Tinsley Wire Industries in Sheffield, where he was groomed for management.

Three years later came his first big chance. He was sent to Durham to take on the job of general manager of a subsidiary firm, a loss-making plant. It says something of his capabilities that he converted it to a profit-making venture. After a five-year stint in the Durham factory he came back to Sheffield, was elevated to the post of Sales Director and afterwards to Group Sales and Marketing Director.

But all was not to his taste. Tinsley dominated the wire market but had grown through acquisition rather than by organic growth. Hugh felt it had become too complacent and too corporate for his taste. On his 38th birthday he left the company to establish his own business, Estate Wires, a company like Tinsley; making fencing wire, mainly for the agricultural market. It was in the capacity of owner-manager of Estate Wire that he first came across the problem facing the Welsh farmer.

The story of the meeting between Hugh and the farmer at the corner of the field has been told and retold over the years but it is not quite what happened. He never met the farmer in person but picked up the story from one of the salesmen just back from Wales.

Don't let the truth get in the way of a good story as they say. But in fact Hugh's real-life story is a matter of the truth being more fascinating than fiction.

For a start, the Gripple story debunks a central tenet of the business school model of what makes for a successful entrepreneur. Most experts on entrepreneurship would have us believe the key skill of the entrepreneur is having the ability to spot opportunities in the marketplace. But that is an oversimplification that omits a key stage in the process. For the successful entrepreneur possesses an unerring ability to sniff out a problem that needs to be solved. The prospective customer may not be even aware that there is a problem until it is pointed out.

In the case of the Welsh farmer, Hugh Facey was very fortunate to have been told the story just as he was setting up his own business and was raring to go. The problem of carrying out repairs on broken fencing without tearing gloves and hands had existed for years without anybody suggesting how this particular form of torture could be eliminated. But

Hugh rose to the challenge. The prize would rest not with the person who spotted the opportunity, but with the person who came up with the answer to the problem. Hugh had a fertile mind and within a few days had conceived of a device that would do the job, if it could be built.

Hugh himself admits that the story of the Welsh farmer made him see the world in a different light: "When I had developed the Gripple and demonstrated how simple and effective it was in joining wires effortlessly, sales just soared and soared. It made me think that there might be other potential customers out there who may not realise they have a problem to solve, and not just farmers. My 20 years of success in building the business from scratch to become a multi-million pound empire, owes as much to that revelation than any other factor."

So the first rule of entrepreneurship is:

$$\begin{array}{c}\textbf{PROBLEM}\\\textbf{SEEKING}\end{array} + \begin{array}{c}\textbf{PROBLEM}\\\textbf{SOLVING}\end{array} = \begin{array}{c}\textbf{CUSTOMER}\\\textbf{GRATITUDE}\end{array} + \textbf{GROWTH}$$

Of course there is much more to starting a successful and growing business than that but it's not a bad place to begin.

Quite apart from his grasp of the dynamics of growing business, Hugh illustrates many of the classic qualities that gave him a flying start into his own business. One is the experience he gained before ever attempting to establish his own business. His five years spent in Durham had given him a grounding in how to lead a business and some understanding of the essentials of finance. It was also proved an introduction to the world of wire manufacture, with a good working knowledge of sales and marketing.

In a sense, you could look at this as an informal apprenticeship in the wire technology, preparing himself for the day when he upped sticks and set up his own wire business. I asked him why he had chosen to leave Tinsley. He told me: "Tinsley was a mature company, one that had grown through mergers and acquisitions. It controlled about 80 percent of the UK market. I didn't feel it was doing enough to find new markets. So I decided to leave and set up my own business."

But to make a success of the business Hugh needed more than cash. He also needed a design engineer. There's a common misconception

that to be an entrepreneur you need to be an inventor. But once you've accepted your own incompetence, you soon realise you can hire a person with the required skills to do the development work. To turn the idea into reality Hugh employed Brian Shawcross, a qualified metallurgist and design engineer who had just given up his job with the NHS because, in his view, it had become too bureaucratic. The NHS's loss was Hugh's gain as he explained: "Brian was recommended to me by people he had worked with. I interviewed him and he showed me examples of his work. He was obviously very competent and I was convinced he could do the job. But I had to be sure we could work together. I spent the morning with him, showing him round the workshop, talking about my idea of how a solution to the broken wire problem might be made to work. I introduced him to the small workforce (at this stage we employed only eight people) and left them all to have a chat. Only when I was absolutely convinced he was the man for the job did we come to discuss terms. He would work two days a week designing and building the Gripple."

"The fact is," Hugh told me, "I have no gift as an inventor. I wouldn't know where to begin. But once I had recruited Brian he could more than make up for my deficiencies. He was the practical man par excellence."

It was Brian's inventive skill that made the Gripple possible. "It took three years to refine the idea into an operator-friendly tool," Brian explained. "Hugh and I discussed the general concept and I came up with a number of possible designs. We tried them out on lengths of wire of different thickness. Hugh was a stickler for making it as simple as possible. Eventually we narrowed it down to two designs and picked the one that worked best in the field. A farmer friend of Hugh let us try it out on a difficult rolling hillside with every conceivable obstacle to its smooth working. Eventually, in 1988, we were ready to launch it on to the market."

But first Hugh and Brian took out a 20-year patent on the design. It was a shrewd move that was repeated again and again as the business developed. It gave them protection against others simply copying their designs.

When the Gripple finally emerged on the market it was an instant success. It was about the size of a small cigarette lighter but made almost

entirely of metal. There were two parallel channels running through the block, each folding back on itself to steer the fence wire round a hairpin to re-emerge close to where it entered. The wires could be tightened up or slackened by means of the allen key. It was instant hit with the farming community. So much so that the original plans to market it had to be changed, as Hugh explained:

"We originally thought of giving a Gripple away free with every roll of wire," Hugh told me. "But we found there was much more demand for the fence- mending machine than there was for the wire. So we simply sold them quite separately from the rolls of wire. They were a sensation."

Fortunately, Estate Wire practically ran itself, and made enough money to pay for the long design process and for the costs of manufacturing. What Hugh did not appreciate was how quickly the Gripple would spawn an army of spin-offs that meant the company could grow and grow. It was a phenomenon closely bound up with Hugh's love of travel and his constant search for new opportunities created by the problems people and companies faced, largely in the business to business market.

The first coup came when someone in the sales team told Hugh about the world's longest animal fence, which straddled the Australian States of Queensland, New South Wales and South Australia, a distance of five thousand kilometres – commonly known as the 'Dingo Fence'. Just where the Australian wild dog came from is still disputed but the damage these roving packs of hungry animals once wreaked on the Australian sheep farmers was huge. Before the fence was erected, over 11,000 sheep and lambs were slaughtered by these ferocious animals in a single year.

The dingo fence dates back to the 1880s and has been controversial ever since. It costs a fortune to maintain and needs constant updating. (The latest threat to it has been the growth in the number of feral camels, animals large enough to push all but the strongest fences down.) The firms who win the contracts to keep it in good order and strong enough to keep the dingoes and camels at bay are under pressure to keep costs to a minimum. This is where the resourceful Hugh struck gold. One of his sales team had heard about the Dingo fence and had a contact number of the head of one of the largest fencing companies – Waratah.

In 1990 he flew off to Australia carrying samples of the Gripple and met up with Bob Foster, the man responsible for putting together a bid for the maintenance and improvement of a third of the fence, about a thousand miles in total.

When they met, Rob and Hugh struck up an immediate rapport. Bob explained that he expected the other bidders would put up a "more of the same" plan that would deliver a fence with all the familiar problems, too easily broken down, very labour intensive, and leaving very little margin for profit.

"I think I have here the solution to your problem," replied Hugh. "This little device would allow us to put up the fence more quickly and make it stronger. It will also require far fewer fence builders. It's called the Gripple."

"The what?"

"The Gripple," said Hugh demonstrating the action with his hands, "because it grips and pulls, but in a very special way." He explained that the company had just produced a new tool to make tensioning of the wire speedier and much more accurate, meaning far less in the way of broken wires or sagging fences. Rob Foster was impressed and asked Hugh how he saw the deal working. Hugh said he'd be happy with an arrangement that left Waratah as the lead contractor, with Gripple slotting in as the exclusive supplier of Gripple technology. It was a dream combination for both the companies: Gripple got a big contract to supply 270 million Gripples and thousands of tensioning machines.

It's a remarkable story, not confined to the Australian market, for the blend of Gripples and tensioning tools has gone on to revolutionise other industries that relied on wire technology. A classic case was the wine industry. Before the Gripple came along the erecting of tressles to support the growing vines was a fairly primitive affair, a very back-breaking business. As the vines grew, new wires were added to provide extra support and the whole structure raised. As the vines grew the stress on the wires increased. Where the wires were corroded -- and many were -- the extra stress led them to break. Putting breakages right and

re-tensioning the vines was a slow and tiring business that took its toll on the vines as well as the vineyard workers.

On a trip to South Africa Hugh was introduced to a vineyard owner who told him about the problem. The Yorkshire entrepreneur was quick to spot the solution. Gripple had been working on the development of high-tension wires that would be galvanised to make them rust-proof. A system based on the new wire and the introduction of a tensioning tool, that gave a precise reading of the stress on the wires, would virtually banish the problem of broken wire and slumping vines. So it came about, thanks to the energetic Hugh, that the Gripple and its tensioning system became established as the world leader in a market that had been made possible by Sheffield ingenuity.

"How had the company managed it?" I asked Hugh.

"Simple really," he told me. "It's all the result of good intelligence on the part of our sales teams, of which I'm part. They keep in regular touch with our customers, personally visiting them and seeing them as colleagues in a joint enterprise. The question they always ask is: "Have you any problems that need solving, have you any special requirements that we can cater for by producing exactly what you want?"

This idea of **problem seeking – problem solving** pervades the company and is written into the company literature.

He read out a paragraph in bold text:

"We pride ourselves on having the wisdom, talent and experience to tackle the issue you face. Send us your problem and we'll see if our design team can offer you a solution – we never say no to a challenge."

We will meet the remarkable Hugh again in Chapter 13 where he describes his unique approach to constantly innovating.

Lessons Learned

At the end of each story I have tried to summarise the key entrepreneurial lessons. The entrepreneurs in this book not only understand the key lessons they live them day-in and day-out. That's what makes them successful in my view.

- Serve an apprenticeship so you learn the lessons at someone else's expense. This significantly reduces the risks and increases the chances of success.

- Find a customer problem and solve it, then sell the solution to everybody else!

- Get a balanced team around you – people who share your values but complement your skills.

- Think global. Where are the big potential customers for your products?

We will see these key lessons appear again and again throughout this book.

On the Trail
of the Code

Hugh Facey has become for me something of a personal hero – a man who makes the role of the entrepreneur seem easy – a piece of cake. It's not at all like that but having a positive attitude to all that the world might throw at you, turning adversity to advantage, sure gives the aspiring entrepreneur a head start. I was not to know this when I started out on a mission to crack the entrepreneurial code 25 years ago. Up to that point I had made quite a mess of my life by any normal measure. Fate had dealt me the short straw, I thought – and marked me out as a loser.

I was born in 1949 into a household that included a father who had been invalided out of the army after going through the hell of Arnhem (a battle immortalised in the film *A Bridge Too Far*) followed by a year in a Nazi prison camp. He was a broken man who spent years in mental hospitals and ended up a drug-dependent wreck. None of this was his fault but it cast a shadow over my early years and left me without the support and advice of a father.

My mother, my younger brother, and I lived in a council house on the eastern outskirts of York – a district called Tang Hall. She was hard-pushed to cope and we boys were left much to our own devices. The only printed material I remember reading was my weekly copy of the Beano. We had no TV so we found our entertainment on the streets or backyards in improvised football and cricket matches. When not doing that we'd be up to some mischief.

Looking back on it I can see that there were only three ways to escape this impoverished backwater: through education, a life of crime, or

by becoming a professional sportsman. The sports option was the one I chose.

Naked before a mirror today it is hard to see myself as the great cricketer I aspired to be. But I was a pretty good batsman and was offered a trial by Yorkshire County Cricket Club. This was a chance of a life-time but I threw it away. It was in part down to bad luck. In the weeks I spent there I fell afoul of a Yorkshire player who was a good batsman. But to me he lacked a sense of humour. He understood the importance of purposeful practice in order to become successful but I did not until later on in life.

When I played with him as a batting partner in a trial match, I made the mistake of calling on him to take a quick single and succeeded in having him run-out. He was furious and gave me a tongue-lashing. I don't think he ever forgot his humiliation. But what proved the last straw was when an elderly woman (as I perceived it as a callow youth) called in to meet him, I ran to the team dressing room and announced that his mother was waiting in the pavilion to see him. Of course his team mates cottoned on immediately that this was not his mother but his girlfriend and burst into peals of laughter. That was the end of my cricketing dream.

By this time I had ruled out the second escape channel, education. I did that by failing to pass my Eleven Plus exam. Passing the Eleven Plus was like being given a golden ticket to Willy Wonka's chocolate factory. The exam separated the sheep from the goats. Those who passed went on to gain entrance to university or to a top technical college. If they were not academically brilliant (and many of those who passed fell into that category) they would at least be offered a respectable career. Those who failed (in York a full 75 percent of the school population) were drafted into the local 'Secondary Modern' schools, generally looked on as schools for dummies. They could look forward to a tradesman job if they were lucky, if unlucky to a low-paid unskilled worker's job, or worse, to casual employment.

I had never given much thought to the Eleven Plus. Nor had my mother. She assumed I was doing all right at school. We never discussed it. But when I presented her with the envelope containing the result, she was utterly shocked. I will never forget the look on her face. I felt I had let her down badly.

It meant I was sent to a very bad school where little or no learning took place. When I approached my 15th birthday I was duly booked in for a 'careers' appointment – something of a farce since the 'advisor', a large lady smelling of mothballs, took one look at me and said "You're a big strapping lad – have you thought about being a plumber?"

I was sent for an interview as an apprentice plumber and unfortunately for me (and for them) I was successful.

The assumption behind the secondary modern was that people who were not good with their heads had a more practical bent. I proved them wrong. At least as far as 'hands' were concerned. My work became the butt of the workshop humour. I spent a miserable four months battling with pipework; a modern day Hercules wrestling with the snake in the form of copper pipes.

Things, I thought, could hardly get worse.

It was during this period of near despair that I sought any consolation I could get – in the pages of glossy climbing magazines. The Hercules of the early 60s was Chris Bonnington. In 1962 he had climbed the north wall of the Eiger in winter and had come back safely. He went on to other great feats including the conquest of two great Himalayan peaks. In 1965 his face was everywhere and he had become something of a national hero. I little knew that one day I was to meet him, shake him by the hand and work with him running leadership programmes! Looking back now of these days of hero worship, I can see that they helped bring about the change in my life I so desperately craved.

Like many of the entrepreneurs I was going to meet I reacted to both negative and positive stimuli. If this sounds a bit sweeping and hi-falutin', I can tell you that 30 years of experience has shown to me again and again that the most successful entrepreneurs have the most negative and positive moments in their life experiences. The mixture seems to somehow strengthen their drive and motivation. The positive in my case came from my Chris Bonnington fixation, the negative from my mother's heartache and disappointment.

Here, I have to confess, I don't know why things turned out as they did.

Did someone in the business who knew of my pile of magazines mention it to a manager? Or did reading the magazines change my outward disposition in a way that would be apparent to the management? Whatever, I was astonished to find myself elevated within the business to the post of junior manager. Charlie Emmerson, the Managing Director of the firm, promoted me because I got a distinction in an exam at the local technical college – in the theory section, not the practical. That was not the end of it. Some weeks after I had made the leap to the ranks of management my manager, a supportive and open-hearted man called Raymond Elderton, called me in and asked if I would like to go on a four-week outward bound course, a test of character that involved a mixture of canoeing, hill-walking and camping in exposed places, centred on Eskdale in the English Lake District. There would be 20 young men on the course, all about by my age. It appealed to my sense of adventure and, inspired by Chris Bonnington, I seized the opportunity to do something exciting.

When we assembled at Eskdale I found myself in a minority of one. The other 19 were mainly the products of English private schools – oddly known as public schools. They were dressed in the right gear and spoke the Queen's English. I was dressed in an anorak and spoke in a hesitant Yorkshire dialect that they found difficult to understand. I couldn't see me lasting the course, but in the end the values we shared outweighed the differences. After two weeks, they and I had overcome the initial problems of communication and were working well together. Nothing was more of a surprise to me than when I was elected leader for the last fortnight. This meant leading a group of ten people on an expedition. We survived, succeeded and I had my first taste of leadership. I came back to York feeling several feet taller. I told everyone that I went a boy and came back a man.

On my return, looking the picture of health, I found that my friendly manager had now signed me up for a 'career assessment'. It meant travelling to Harley Street in London on my own, my first visit to the capital. In my new incarnation as a self-assured young Yorkshireman, I tackled this fancy new type of testing. It assessed personality and aptitude, using what is now established and accepted techniques, though not so well-known or trusted in the early 70s. I was called into the examiner's

office to assess the results. "Well, Mr Hall, we have a very interesting set of outcomes," he said. "You are clearly wasting your talents in your present job. Our advice is to give up a career in plumbing." This was hardly a ground-breaking revelation. But then came the interesting stuff. "You told us you had never excelled in communicating or in leading teams of people. But these results just don't match your opinion of yourself. You have fine communication skills, and good leadership potential."

"So what type of job do you think I'd be best suited for?" I asked. I was flabbergasted when the tester replied: "You should think of something like being a lawyer, or a journalist, or a management consultant."

On the way back up to York I had a chance to mull over the options. The idea of parading in a wig and robe just did not appeal to me, too much like play-acting. On the other hand, jobs in journalism were hard to come by, especially jobs in what was regarded as quality journalism. Before we had reached York I had made up my mind – I would go for broke for a career in management consultancy – it was relatively easy to find a place on a course run by some of the newer universities, grants were available, and I could take a day job and a night job (how things have changed!) to pay the mortgage and keep cash flowing.

That was the path I now took, picking up my A levels at night school and winning acceptance on to a postgraduate diploma in management course, followed by a Master's Degree in management. I read every business book I could get my hands on and deliberately set out to meet and learn from numerous entrepreneurs whom I found fascinating. I got married for the first time and drove my wife to near despair as an obsessive search for knowledge took over my life. We soon had three kids although, I am ashamed to say, the parenting was delegated largely to my wife. But by God, it was an exciting time for me!

Over the next ten years my business grew at a breathtaking speed, perhaps a reflection of my energy and my never-say-die attitude. That's at least how I saw it. By the end of the 1980s my company had opened 14 offices across the North of England and was employing 150 carefully chosen staff. It was a matter of some pride, although I can see the availability

of public money to fund business training played a big part. You have to remember the background. In Yorkshire and the North, the 1980s had suffered a widespread cull of the traditional heavy industries, such as steel and heavy engineering, to be followed by the miners' strike and the virtual end of coal mining in territory long-dependent on 'King Coal'. Thousands of people were thrown out of work. The hope was that new industries would rise to take up the slack. To help this process, 'enterprise agencies' were set up to help retrain redundant workers and to find men and women with entrepreneurial talent who would employ them.

Get these talented people going – so the theory went – and Britain could once again become the workshop of the world. But just where were these paragons to come from, and who would train them in the art of running a business?

I was interested in both questions. One of the country's leading centres in business training for start-up businesses was at Durham University. In 1989 they were running a programme for entrepreneurs who wanted to expand their businesses and needed a helping hand. I was invited to travel from my new base in Doncaster to contribute to their 'growth programme'.

It was to be a turning point in my career. I got to meet Allan Gibb, the professor at the head of Europe's very first Small Business Centre at Durham University. After the two-hour session, he and I relaxed over a pint of Newcastle brown ale. I decided to raise one of my chief concerns about the way business schools and training companies were approaching the task. The textbooks and others materials used on the courses were meant not for start-up companies but for large established businesses. The start-up students' eyes glazed over. I told Allan that everyone shared my opinion but were afraid to speak up. It was a case of the Emperor's new clothes. He agreed and challenged me to do something about it. The rest of this book is the story of my journey to discover how entrepreneurs really do create successful businesses.

What made me think I could crack the entrepreneurial code?

I was an entrepreneur myself so I was living the dream personally;

My passion from an early age, initially with mountain climbers, was for the brave bold people who take risks and achieve great things;

My work as a consultant was with entrepreneurs. I lived and work with them every day. I signed up for a PhD at Lancaster University and spent two years studying research methods so I knew how to conduct research with entrepreneurs in a disciplined manner. Finally, I was prepared to invest my time and money into researching how entrepreneurs create success.

However, I am not an academic researcher, but somebody who is interested in finding out answers to problems. So I hired the very best people I could find who had the skills and experiences that I did not possess in order to help me to crack the code. You will meet them all in this book.

Why am I so passionate about the cause of entrepreneurs?

I was immersed in the entrepreneurial process so I understood their dilemmas, hopes and dreams. This work, which has been researched over a period of 25 years, has at its core a passionate ambition to explain just how people can start businesses successfully, how companies can grow and become major employers, while at the same time becoming a reservoir of ideas and skills that turn a growing company into a beacon of innovation. If enough of them are successful then the economy can grow and the world might become a better place. That was my challenge.

So settle down and find out how I fared.

Lessons Learned

- When you get a once-in-a-lifetime opportunity (like playing for the Yorkshire cricket team) you should take it seriously. I deeply regret I didn't do this.

- Find out what you are good at and build on this through career guidance. I ensured all my children had career guidance which has served them well.

- Find a work/life balance – children grow up far too quickly and I wish I had been more involved. I try harder with my grandchildren not to repeat past mistakes.

- Try to learn from the people who are the best in their field – don't compromise!

- Find people who can help you, that have skills and competences that complement your own.

- Try to find a purpose in life that really inspires you – mine has been cracking the code. What will your legacy be?

The Dog Hotel and Phileas Fogg

The conversation I had with Allan Gibb at Durham University in late 1989 completely changed the course of my life. Before we began the research into what makes the entrepreneur tick, I had initially pursued a career as a business consultant, teaching the academic texts and conducting the standardised exercises, helping to create a picture of how business organisations operate and survive in a fiercely competitive world. When it came to courses for the small business sector, we simply boiled down the knowledge that big businesses had taken years to acquire into easily digested portions – a bit like trying to cram fifty quarts into a pint pot. I was getting very concerned that we were not really helping small businesses…

When the entrepreneurs completed the course (**IF** they completed the course) they were vastly overloaded with information, much of which they had little chance to put into practice, at least until the knowledge had become outdated or forgotten. Let me mention here just one feature of the conventional training programmes. They were all based on what is today termed 'rational activity' – logically organised, strictly procedural and profoundly analytical. In some countries – such as Japan – there has been much more emphasis on 'creative activity', the use of knowledge that stemmed from traditional wisdom, or intuitive learning. Western countries have been slow to adopt methods that tap into these powerful human capabilities, too long neglected.

When we later began our research programme into entrepreneurial success we were struck by the use of creative skills. It only served to highlight the quite different techniques employed by the entrepreneur.

But I digress.... First we need to meet and then follow Dinah Bennett on her quest, a quest that I found myself increasingly drawn into. We recruited Dinah who was a bright young woman but deliberately with no entrepreneurial experience. We did not want to taint or influence the research process.

Dinah and I began by making a selection from the 'top sixty' small businesses supplied by Durham Business School. This list was whittled down to just 30 individual entrepreneurs on the basis of Dinah's initial interviews. She arranged to go and see them in action and to follow their progress over a period of 2 years.

Dinah interviewed the lead entrepreneur at each business and discussed how they dealt with the challenges small companies face day to day. Her findings were then discussed by the team at Durham University under the leadership of Allan Gibb and myself. We must have chosen well as ten years later twenty eight out of the thirty businesses chosen in 1989 were still in existence.

We began by devising questions about that all-important factor in small business survival and growth – the customer. We were surprised to find that many of our entrepreneurs saw **solving the problems of the customer** as a key factor in long-term growth. Even stranger was how often the link with problem-solving went back to the personal experience of the new entrepreneurs as consumers themselves.

I must stress here that the lessons we learned from the Hallmarks research came from many of the thirty companies we researched, not just one or two. We were looking for patterns of behaviour among entrepreneurs that seemed to lead to success. We concluded that entrepreneurs learned far more effectively by looking at real-life problems and coming up with solutions rather than taking theoretical examples. Entrepreneurs prefer to get their wisdom from successful peers, not books.

So with this in mind let me introduce you to Ann Adlington, one of our Hallmarks companies.

When Dinah first met Ann Adlington she knew she was onto a winner. Ann had spent 20 years working as a nurse. She had a caring streak

running deeply through her very being, allied to a pragmatic Geordie tendency to call a spade a spade (and that's putting it politely).

In 1981 she and her husband, Arthur, had booked a holiday in the States and needed to find a place to kennel their three large and exuberant Afghan Hounds. "We were very worried that we might leave the dogs with someone who laid on a minimum service, and would not be able to handle these loving but large animals. We worried about it so much that we visited 17 boarding kennels and couldn't find one we considered up to scratch. In the end Arthur and I had to leave them with my mother."

The trauma was still with them when they boarded the plane.

The experience made them think. If we can't find decent kennels for our dogs, there must be hundreds of other people in the same plight. Could we build a business here in the North East where people would be glad to quarter their dogs? "I know it sounds sentimental," said Ann, "but I couldn't simply leave the dogs with people who didn't care about them. They deserved the same standard of attention and pampering care that we give to humans."

What perhaps clinched the argument in favour of setting up a new business was Ann's research. "Arthur and I attended a conference in the USA run by the American Kennels Association. There were thousands of people and dogs there. We discovered that people were offering all sorts of services to dogs and cats just like they do for human beings. Swimming lessons, acupuncture, aerobics for dogs, grooming, even dog counselling – it was amazing!"

Bizarre it might sound, but here was a brilliant new business opportunity served up on a dog platter. As soon as Ann got back to Britain she developed her vision of this luxury hotel for cats and dogs.

"We looked for an appropriate site. Eventually we found a 10-acre site in the middle of nowhere, a derelict farm. We decided to offer a whole range of services in one place and in the winter of 1982 Triple 'A' Ranch was born."

From day one, the idea was a hit. Over the next 20 years the business expanded until there were three Triple A Ranches employing a staff of over 100, fully trained by Ann.

How was it financed? Apart from an initial loan from her bank, Triple A Ranch was entirely self-financing. This was because the "Ranch" charged fees for care that were three times higher than her rivals.

Even at that price the customers considered it money well spent (the level of re-bookings was uniquely high at 98 percent!).

What Ann did was to change a commodity (a dog's kennel complex) into a luxury holiday home for pets, cleverly transforming human guilt into a great experience for dogs and extra cash.

Delighting Customers Pays Dividends
Why could Ann charge so much more than her competitors? Well this is what you get for your money, judge for yourself:

• Themed kennels with a sofa and bed
• 4 walks per day
• Daily grooming

Extras include:

• 'Cuddles' contact
• Massage
• Aerobics
• Acupuncture
• Swimming pool for dog exercise
• Phone calls to owners on the dog's progress while on holiday

When the owner gets home there is a postcard from the dog saying it had a great time and when are you going away again! The key lesson is that nothing needs to be a commodity, something so common and universal that it sells for rock bottom prices. You can add value to any service; it just requires imagination and innovation.

Ann also took responsibility for the industry – a key factor in highly successful entrepreneurs. Back in 1982 there was no proper training for people working in domestic animal care so Ann created a professional qualification and paid for over 100 people to be properly trained.

The American giant Mars (the food group) asked Ann to develop her concept so they could take it worldwide. She sold her business to Mars in 2001 and stayed on as a consultant. After 12 months she left to set up *Coarse Fishing Lakes* called Angel of the North Fishing Lakes, along with livery yard and arable land for future developments.

Postscript: The business is now called 'MyPetsStop'.

What are the lessons from the Ann Adlington case?

Find a problem you are really passionate about.

Create a solution based upon best practice from wherever you can find it in the world.

Don't just be different, be better!

Set out to delight your customers – dogs and owners in this case.

If you do all of the above really well your reward is you can charge premium prices.

> "The lesson from Ann Adlington is that nothing needs to be a commodity, you can add value to anything if you have a vision and a passion to succeed. If Anne can do it with dog kennels what can you do with your business?"
>
> *Professor Allan Gibb*

With people like Ann around – focused on solving the problems of the customer – any new business is off to a flying start, maximising its chances of success. As Ann's experience with Mars Brothers shows, when one door closes another opens.

The findings of our research study proved to be quite staggering – and not just in relation to traditional customers. The findings became the basis of a new training programme for entrepreneurs and have been adopted in America, South Africa, Australia and Croatia – the Hallmarks System.

But before we leave it, we should consider a second lesson that we drew from the Durham based project. We showed that new businesses don't always spring up to keep existing customers happy. They can create new categories of products, and entirely new markets where none existed before.

To show what I mean, let's have a look at another Hallmarks hero, Roger McKechnie of Derwent Valley Foods. Entrepreneurs don't just appear out of the ether bringing nothing but their wits and personalities. At least very few do. They come with a back story, which can be highly significant.

Roger McKechnie was one of these entrepreneurs. There was no history of enterprise in his family and he seemed quite happy to be employed as a well-paid marketing man initially with Proctor and Gamble and later with General Mills and Associated Biscuits until he was asked to move south to London at the age of forty. He refused, saying he was emotionally attached to the North-East and he wanted to stay there.

It meant leaving his role as Managing Director of Tudor Crisps (an AB Subsidiary) but he left holding a valuable asset, years of training in marketing. He told me: "Proctor and Gamble was renowned as a firm that was strong in marketing. I got a good grounding and came to understand how clever marketing could underpin a switch into new markets."

As it happened he had been in charge of the marketing and production of Tudor Crisps, a long famous potato crisp sold to children as school-break snacks. He had been keeping an eye on overseas developments in snack foods: "I had noticed how tortilla chips had become popular in the States and were being sold at a much higher price to adults. When I chose to pack up and leave P&G I already had the idea of creating a new kind of snack food that we could sell at a premium price to the adult market."

He lived just outside of Durham and knew it would be easy to find a factory on the new industrial estate at Consett, set up to create jobs to replace those lost with the closure of the Consett Iron works in 1981.

In 1982 it was a great place to start a business. The local enterprise agencies were desperate for new businesses to move in. "They were even advertising on Metro Radio for people with ideas, any kind of ideas, to come to the town," he said. He recruited a partner, Keith Gill, a former employee at Tudor Crisps, a man with a head for figures who could keep the somewhat chaotic Roger under control.

With only the vaguest idea of the product to be made, they drew up a business plan on the back of a fag packet and took it to the people who were leasing out premises.

"They went for it. Even better, they helped us find most of the starting capital we needed. We could go straight into business."

Looking over the site of the old steelworks, Roger could see it was more than adequate for the job even if it was no more than an unglamorous shed. The exotic new fries and snacks could be made and packaged in just one corner of the building before being dispatched to customers.

It helped that Roger had a vision that excited the keen new recruits. He produced his drawings and recipes for the range of snacks and was commissioning the design for his eye-catching packaging.

"This was the most important aspect of the plan," he stressed, "we needed to invent a brand name that suggested an exotic food, with a hint of continental sophistication fit to grace any middle-class party. What I had in mind was a range of products that would attract attention anywhere in the world. Then I suddenly got it. We took the Jules Verne character, Phileas Fogg, and gave his name to our snacks. Fogg was famous as the explorer (fictional of course) who had flown round the world in a balloon in 80 days, and therefore had the necessary international appeal.

All that was needed were the fryers, the oils and spices and a professional cook. They then needed to prepare the right kind of marketing exercise. The small team multi-tasked, acting as delivery van drivers three days a week, and managers, intelligence gatherers, and general dogs bodies for the rest of the week.

There's not enough room here to detail all the ruses that were used – although the notion of Consett having an international airport on Medomsley Road, a down-at-the-heel and pot-holed mess, was one that put a smile on people's faces.

With his Croutons, Tortilla Chips, Mignons, and other snacks, selling like hot-cakes, retailing at four times the price of crisps, Roger was soon smiling all the way to the bank.

Roger had created a new market where before there had been none, and at minimum cost. It was a niche market, an opportunity the big boys had missed, to their cost.

Twelve years later Roger sold the business for £24 million pounds, showing that small business can flourish while the giants slumber.

There is one feature of the Roger McKechnie story that's very common in start-up businesses. Roger was in essence a refugee from big business who made off to found his own company, taking with him not only good employees but people with very valuable skills. He had in a sense served an apprenticeship and earned his spurs long before Phileas Fogg ever landed at Medomsley Road airport.

Did You Know?

50% of entrepreneurs with a record of growth are people who have served an apprenticeship with a large corporate business for at least 10 years. In that time they learn their trade at somebody else's expense. When they get disheartened by the slow pace in decision making found in many bigger companies, or get stifled by layers of bureaucracy, they often leave to set up their own business.

Roger's Advice to Entrepreneurs

Get a good team around you with complementary skills.

Look for gaps in the market that you can exploit, particularly where new trends are emerging.

Be ethical in all you do. "I get really upset by people who do not behave in the right way. In the old days a person's word was their bond – not anymore!" he said.

Most of all have fun and enjoy it, and if you can't then do something else!

Roger's Genius

Roger has started a number of successful businesses since he sold Derwent Valley Foods but it was his genius in recognising an opportunity to create a new market that made him a great entrepreneur.

Five things you should do if you can:
Serve an 'apprenticeship' in your industry of choice, learning the ropes at somebody else's expense.

Get a balanced team around you by understanding your strengths and weaknesses and getting people who share your values and complement your skills.

Be on the lookout for changing customer behaviours and wants – these may be opportunities. A clue is to look what is happening around the world …

Establish a clear personality for your business – your brand.

Once again, if you do all that well you can charge premium prices!

Both Ann Adlington and Roger McKechnie were part of our original Hallmarks study conducted by Dinah Bennett.

Our Hallmarks study with 30 successful North East of England companies was developed into a business development approach:

1. Focus and Direction	Design and manage the focus and direction of the business.
2. Customerising	Continually delight customers in order to get repeat business, referrals and a lowering of sensitivity to price.
3. Partnering	Work in partnership with people who affect your business.
4. Personality	Manage the culture of the business.
5. Competitiveness	Build a sustainable competitive advantage.
6. Systems	Establish systems and processes that enable people to manage the business effectively.

See *The Hallmarks of Successful Business*, Management Books 2000 for more details.

From this a three day training programme was devised for growth businesses and several thousand companies have been trained in the Hallmarks model since 1993.

In 1992 The British Television Service, the BBC asked me to turn the Hallmarks programme into a TV series which we called 'Winning'. This featured the key Hallmarks lessons in a six part series which won a Royal Television Society BAFTA, thanks mainly to the outstanding production team.

Has the Hallmarks worked? Do Hallmarks companies grow successfully as our research predicted?

In 2000, 10 years after the Hallmarks programmes were launched, an independent review was undertaken by John Lupton of Sheffield University. He personally interviewed 75 businesses who had completed the programme. He found that over 47 percent reported a considerable improvement in generating new business. 54 percent had a greater customer commitment and profits had improved significantly in 52 percent of the companies.

Dr Tim Mazzarol of Curtin Business School in Perth Australia evaluated the performance of 98 businesses who had attended Hallmarks programmes in Perth. His study found *a significant relationship between high sales growth and the key Hallmarks.*

- A stronger level of customer commitment
- A commitment to partnering
- Good cash flow
- A commitment to action
- Strong and sustainable competitive advantage

The Hallmarks programme has been delivered in Romania, Croatia, Australia, and South Africa and was reviewed by Dinah Bennett of Durham Business School. Her conclusion was *"These models seem to make sense to business people across cultures. They value their practical, comprehensive, yet simple way of communicating complex issues."*

Unfortunately, although we now know a lot more about how small entrepreneurial businesses grow successfully, many business schools, consultants and advisors are still promoting the traditional stuff. It's a bit like going to a doctor who then puts leeches on your arm to cure

a disease just as he would have done 100 years ago, or ships at sea still trying to communicate with flags!

We will be looking later at why start-up businesses produce so many of the new ideas for businesses of all types, be it manufacturing, services, and IT but our next research study of Scottish entrepreneurs did throw up a fascinating case of two entrepreneurs who created a completely new market from scratch.

Benefits of delighting customers:
- High levels of repeat business.
- New business from referrals from delighted customers.
- Lowering of sensitivity to price.

Lessons Learned
- Don't just be different, be much, much better.
- Find something you are really passionate about.
- Seek to find a gap in the market.
- Build a strong brand that's on everyone's lips.
- Spend time networking with the right people. It's *'know who, not know how'*. Networking has been shown to have the highest correlation with successful business growth. So as one Hallmark company said, 'JFDI!'
- Get close to customers in order to identify their real problems and offer to solve them. Problem-seeking and problem-solving is the way that ALL entrepreneurs create superior business opportunities. Then sell the solution to the world!
- Seek to delight customers. Go the extra mile; really surprise them with your level of support and service.
- Create long-term, mutually-beneficial, customer partnerships based on trust and integrity.
- Build a team with complementary skills. Don't try to do it all yourself.

As we have seen, the Hallmarks research was hailed as a breakthrough study of entrepreneurs in action, but those at the centre of the Durham study knew it represented only a modest move forward. Businesses were established and survived for years, but few of them ever grew into companies employing more than ten people. There was still something lacking about our knowledge of entrepreneurs – the entrepreneurial code – or as I now called it – the **entre**code® – had still to be deciphered.

The next step in the journey was to take us north of the border to Scotland.

Code Hunting in Scotland

In 1990 any motorist driving round the head of Loch Fyne in the Argyll district of Scotland risked being met by a strange ritual – a man in a wet suit wading out of the clear waters of the sea loch carrying a large basket full of oysters. Back from the shore was a large eatery where passing tourists could dine on these magnificent molluscs fresh from the sea, washed down with a glass of dry white wine. The story behind Loch Fyne Oysters is a glorious tale of how two dedicated entrepreneurs created a whole new industry on the west coast of highland Scotland.

The entrepreneurs who brought the oyster industry to these rocky shores first met in 1977. They were John Noble (known as Johnny), a man who knew absolutely nothing about farming oysters but knew something of the London appetite for this prince of shell-fish, and Andy Lane, a marine biologist who lived a near hermit's life on the banks of the long arm of the sea that was Loch Fyne.

Andy was driven by the need to make some money. One day he hoped to get married. That couldn't be done on the wages of an odd job man. For Johnny Noble, who was an old Etonian and regarded as being comfortably off, ideas for making money were even more pressing. His father had died five years previously leaving behind massive debts, and though Johnny did his best to keep up appearances, he was battling to keep himself afloat. The debts, secured against the family stately home at the head of Loch Fyne, continued to mount, and large death duties remained to be paid. Out of such adversity arose a brand new industry with long-term prospects of growth – one day it may rise to rival that of France.

But before we follow the remarkable story of Johnny Noble and Andy Lane, we need to wind the spool on to 1992. By that time news of the Hallmarks research findings had spread across Scotland. We had shown that there were patterns that marked out "high growth" entrepreneurs, patterns that could be documented and turned into guides to best practice. But we had a long way to go before we could say we really understood what went on in the heads of entrepreneurs at the moment of inspiration and how they went about building the capability to support the business while it expanded.

The road ahead, as the story of Johnny and Andy shows us, is almost certain to be rocky one, but good entrepreneurs see this as part of the challenge. Successfully growing a two man business (or a two woman business for that matter) means navigating the hazards that lie ahead as the small start-up business grows to become a larger and larger one. Johnny and Andy are as good an example you can find of how determination and resilience can find a way to tackle the many problems that lie ahead.

Soon after the publication of Hallmarks (my study of North of England Entrepreneurs) I was approached by the head of strategy at Scottish Enterprise, Dr Brian McVey, to see if I would conduct a similar piece of research on Scotland and recommend what steps were needed to develop the high growth businesses Scotland so desperately needed to take the place of its traditional heavy industry. The truth was that the Scottish record of new job creation was very poor, and Scottish Enterprise, a body charged with bringing new businesses north of the border had virtually nothing to show for all the energy and resources they had expended.

I accepted the commission and started work with a list of twelve new Scottish companies, firms that in Brian's opinion seemed to have mastered the trick of expansion and growth. Johnny Noble was one of the names on the list so I travelled north to Glasgow and north again to the lonely and beautiful Loch Fyne.

Johnny didn't seem a typical entrepreneur, more of an eccentric country gentleman, but he had a fascinating story to tell with just the hint of a stutter that an education at Eton had not extinguished. "My father owned the 12,000- hectare Ardkinglas estate on the shores of Loch

Fyne in the Scottish Highlands. When he died in 1972 he left me a massive headache, a huge debt to the bank secured against Ardkinglas House. Where could we possibly find the means of repaying these debts without selling the house itself, which I was determined not to do? It was designed and built by a very famous Scottish architect and I felt it was my duty to keep it in the family.

"On the land itself we had some forestry and sheep-farming but that didn't make much money, not enough to settle the debts or even make a profit. As for tourism, it was on a pretty small scale and seasonal. That left only the clear waters of Loch Fyne. Maybe they could build a fish farm like the many that were spreading in the sheltered waters further north?"

It was now 1975 and Johnny was still borrowing money from the bank, making the need to find a profitable venture ever more urgent. One day that autumn as he walked along the shore he met the man who was to help him achieve the impossible. Bent over an assembly of zinc tanks brimful with fresh water from a little mountain stream was a figure dressed in a warm jumper. This was Andy Lane, a marine biologist by training, checking out the tanks full of unpolluted fresh water.

He looked up and recognised the newcomer as the laird of Ardkinglas, Johnny Noble. "How is the hatchery coming on?" asked the tweed-suited laird as a way of breaking the ice."

"These are the young salmon, the par, just three days old," the younger man explained. "After a year they'll be big enough to put in the cages." Soon the two men were utterly engrossed in a long conversation.

Johnny had come to the conclusion that a salmon farm might be the answer to his problem. Andy, with his cloth cap pushed back over his forehead, quickly disabused him of the idea. He had come to the West Highlands hoping to find that fish farming might save the wild salmon. But now, he bleakly explained, pollution and the overuse of chemical treatments to control the spread of sea lice, had made fish farming a grizzly business and a danger to wild fish. He spoke with conviction as he worked as a diver, being lowered into the salmon cages to recover dead fish. It was a never-ending task.

So if fish farming was ruled out what was left?

Andy had an idea. Only the day before, he had been talking to three men in a pub in Ardfern, 30 miles to the west. They had lain out a man-made oyster bed, but with very unhappy results. The oysters had grown extremely slowly and were of very poor quality. Andy guessed right away that these rooky oystermen had made an elementary error. They had built their oyster beds in tidal water deep enough to keep the sacks of growing molluscs fully covered at low tide. This was an elementary blunder, enough to explain the poor outcome. Oysters tighten their shells as the sea retreats, and relax them when the water rises again to cover them. This exercise, Andy explained, makes them more muscular and better tasting.

So was an Oyster farm feasible in Loch Fyne?

Johnny knew from his youth that there had once been wild oysters growing here. In fact, as a boy, he had been sent to gather their empty shells on the shore and take them back to the big house where they were ground down and mixed into the feed for the hens.

It then emerged that Johnny had another asset that would help get a new business off the ground. He had some experience of the main market for expensive shellfish, the restaurants in London. He knew from spending time with his old Etonian friends how much the oyster had been elevated to a fashionable dinner table item, fresh from the sea, full of vitamins, and with an enviable reputation as an aphrodisiac. He could depend on his old school pals acting as unpaid ambassadors in London.

While the two grew more enthusiastic and easier in each other's company, they could also see the risks. What if the shellfish didn't flourish and failed to reach maturity? A mortality rate of ten percent might produce a viable crop, whereas twenty percent could mean certain failure.

Another unanswerable question: Would there be enough plankton in the sea loch to maximise the chances of survival?

More immediate was the problem of getting the shellfish to London in fresh condition. Loch Fyne was nigh on 500 miles from London. Was there some way to deliver the oysters to London on time and at a reasonable cost?

And then there was the awkward but inescapable fact that it took four years for oysters to mature. How could the first four years of outlay, with no income to speak of, be funded? Both felt it was time to do what Andy described as a feasibility study.

They started with some advantages. Andy was a marine biologist and had a fair grasp of the life-cycle of the oyster and indeed of shellfish in general. He was also a much more businesslike person than Johnny, armed not only with a useful degree but with a gift for practical work. While his partner was gauche and cack-handed, Andy could turn his hand to most things. It was therefore a good sign when Johnny quite happily left Andy to do the feasibility study. Andy tried to answer basic questions. For a start, where would the seed oysters come from? His thinking here was governed by a lack of oyster farmers in Britain. To find the best oysters available in 1997 – without the help of the Internet – was going to be difficult. France, and particularly Brittany, might offer the best prospects. More research was needed with some low-cost tests of different seed oysters. Perhaps sending Andy to France could be considered. Meanwhile, as a test-run, some oyster seed could be bought from a small oyster hatchery in Loch Creran, north of Oban.

The wooden trestles for supporting the bags of maturing oysters could be made on site at Loch Fyne. Andy knew exactly what would be required and he could build them himself, with help from the estate workers. As for getting the fresh oysters to London, Andy had soon worked out they could be carried by rail from Arrochar-Tarbet station on the old West Highland Line. To reach it would involve hiring a van to carry the shellfish over the Rest and Be Thankful Pass, a route rising to 300 metres but usually free of winter snows. Once on the train, British Rail would undertake to deliver the day's order to London restaurants in time for lunch.

The old buildings at Ardkinglas House would be used to house young oysters, while Johnny's motor boat would serve as makeshift transport to carry the oyster gatherers out over the loch to allow inspection. A rubber dinghy, albeit with a hole in it, could serve as a back-up.

It all seemed to add up. There was risk enough, but a risk worth taking. But there remained the thorny question of how it was to be financed.

Reluctantly, Johnny revealed there was always the option of raising another loan from the banks (at the cost of increasing the Noble debt) or making an application to the state-funded Highland and Islands Development Board for launch support. Andy's projections suggested there would be a profit, but not for four years. They decided to go for it, though it took several weeks to take that leap.

Johnny wrote out a partnership agreement and both signed it. Loch Fyne Oysters was born. Andy put in his week's notice at the salmon farm and emerged with the title of Managing Director, Loch Fyne Oysters. He promptly went on the dole and managed to support himself with the help of Her Majesty's Government for that first crucial period when he had no other income of any kind.

The first task was to make a test. Andy ordered some seed oysters from Loch Creran hatchery which were duly delivered and placed in their sacking on the trestles at the head of the Loch. They waited for four months to assess the crop. The outcome was very disappointing. It turned out that the Loch Creran had been exposed to a poisonous anti-fouling paint used to clear ships of weed. This batch of oysters would never sell.

There was no alternative but to try again. This time Johnny paid for Andy to go to Brittany in search of oyster seed. Because of his wine business he had contacts there and they gave Andy a warm welcome. He collected new seed oysters and in his best French exchanged information on how to get the best results. He returned to Loch Fyne with the precious stock and laid out the new oysters for a second try.

By this time, 1978, the finances were being severely strained. So they formally established a limited company with a 50-50 division of the shares and turned to the Highlands and Island Development Board for launch aid. It was hard and tedious work, involving long hours of writing a full business plan – a formality they had to go through just to be considered for help. They brushed down the feasibility study and brought it fancifully up to date. Then they held their breath, hoping they would qualify, worrying that they might not.

Eventually, after what seemed an age, the deputy chairman of the board travelled from Inverness to inspect the site. He muttered something about

using the latest technology – a sticky tape to hold the oysters together above the floor of the loch. Andy scarcely concealed his irritation.

But the HIDB came up trumps. It awarded them a grant of £30,000 plus a soft loan to the same value, £60,000 in hard cash. For the moment at least the crisis was over.

What could they do as they waited for the oyster crop to mature? Andy reckoned Loch Fyne would be a great place to raise some rainbow trout. They would produce quick returns and help conserve the company resources. So they plunged in. Andy, assisted by their first employee, David Weir, bought some cages and assembled them in the waters of Loch Fyne. The young fish would have to survive their first and only winter, but in the west of Scotland winters are usually mild. Unfortunately, 1979 proved an exception. Loch Fyne froze over for weeks on end, the ice wrecked the cages, and the fish escaped.

Only the insurance money paid on the wrecked cages saved the day. In 1980 they made another attempt. Amazingly, a second cold winter followed the first. This time there was no insurance money. And David Weir's wages had to be paid. Only the grant was left, and some of that had already been spent on Andy's trip to France. To keep the company going, Johnny had to dip into his pocket yet again. Andy Lane helped ease the pain a little by reducing his share of the company to 40 percent, donating 10 percent of his shares to Johnny.

It is worth pausing at this point to consider the lessons to be learnt so far. There are three very obvious ones. The first concerns the choice of a business partner. People hoping to set up business often feel more secure if they can form a partnership with a colleague or even some long-standing friend. While an emotional bond between partners can be useful in stressful times it is not usually so. The biggest mistake of the would-be entrepreneur is to choose a partner who has the same range of skills and contacts as they have. In the case of Johnny and Andy we have two very different sorts of people. Johnny was an extroverted old Etonian, who had lived in London and mixed with old school friends. He was a confident man, even if a slight stutter suggests there may have been some trauma in his youth. In the context of Argyll he was well-known and

respected. He had the aura of leadership thrust upon him, insofar as was a Laird – a Scottish landed gentleman. He was a born marketer, sociable, persuasive, and with a tendency to open too many bottles of French wine. When it came to doing anything practical he was a washout. He wasn't 'good with his dabs', and not much better at running a business from day to day.

Andy Lane was in many ways his opposite. He was born into a working class family in Nottinghamshire and won a scholarship to Laxton School, which he attended as a 'day boy'. His school merged with Oundle. He appears to have viewed 'public school' education with mixed emotions. He has written: *It was an eye-opener, going to a public school and seeing the feet of clay of people that my aunt and great aunts, the domestic servants, would have thought as their betters. Seeing it clearly.*

When he graduated he wanted to get away from it all, and jumped at the chance when he was offered a job on a salmon farm. He was in so many ways the perfect foil for Johnny Noble. Andy was disillusioned with his first employer, a salmon farm that was owned by remote shareholders and where everyone felt expendable. He was dying to find a way out, especially if it was related to the sea. He had a high degree of expertise on fishery and was, as we've seen, an excellent odd-job man. He even had passable French. He was just the sort of man that could be sent off to France to gather intelligence of oyster farming methods. He was to select the large Northern Pacific Oyster (the Rock Oyster) as the one most likely to flourish in Loch Fyne. He had a business brain too, though not one concerned with accountancy. In his own way he could inspire people but he was not a natural leader of a growing business. He preferred to live in the shadow of Johnny.

So lesson one is to choose carefully your partner, those you would want to associate with and especially someone with a shared vision – but with complementary skills.

The second lesson concerns the 'rocky road' that all entrepreneurs have to endure and learn to overcome. The example of the failed rainbow trout experiment is a classic. If setbacks in starting up a business are certain to be part of the entrepreneurial experience, persistence is universally a

vital element in overcoming these hurdles. The ability to recover from setbacks is a critical entrepreneurial requirement.

The third lesson concerns the methodology of entrepreneurs. Paper schemes never work. It is only by trial and error that they are able to decide the best course to follow. Thus the year spent waiting to see if the oysters would grow was not a full-scale trial. A series of small trials to work out what is practical and what is not has saved many a new business. Entrepreneurs value action taking, with short feedback loops so they can learn and move on.

Johnny's strength, and his main contribution to the business, was his unerring gift for publicity and cheap PR. He didn't worry about making a fool of himself to get a good line in a national newspaper. On one occasion he set up a barrow on a Knightsbridge pavement and – dressed in a kilt and full highland regalia – sold samples of his products to the passing public. But on other occasions he was more subtle. He knew there were holidaymakers from London who came to stay on the Ardkinglas Estate every summer and that some of them were journalists and foodies.

He invited them round in batches for dinner, produced some samples of his oysters and invited them to try them. He left it to their journalistic nosiness to do the rest. In due course glowing articles about the food and the warm Highland welcome appeared in the London press.

At other times he was more direct. After the opening of the first of the restaurants, the Oyster Bar at Loch Fyne, he invited many of Britain's food writers to come for a free weekend. They included Jane Grigson of the *Observer*, Derek Cooper of the BBC, Fay Maschler of the *Evening Standard*, and, incongruously, David Sheppard, ex-cricketer and the Bishop of Liverpool.

As they sampled the fresh sea food, washed down with glasses of superb Scotch, Johnny regaled them on why Loch Fyne oysters were the finest in Britain, nay indeed, in the world. It helped that Andy had successfully found a way of rearing the large pacific oyster to perfection. In due course, a steady stream of articles appeared in the press, praising the product and the food to the world.

On another occasion he staged a stunt that caught the imagination of the press. A good friend of his, Sir Charles Maclean, owner of the Creggans Inn at Strachur, regularly presided there over a gathering of the Walrus Club. On one occasion, Johnny Noble arranged for oysters to be supplied for that merry gathering.

Afterwards, a mischievous article appeared in the national press, a story picked up on TV and radio, suggesting the club had been formed to bring back Walruses into Loch Fyne. The columnist reported that the last Walrus had been sighted in the Loch as recently as 1846. MacLean himself was quoted as the man backing a scheme to reintroduce the Walrus. It would be good for the diversity of life in the Loch and certainly good for tourism. Johnny Noble replied with fake outrage that these creatures could dispose of 6,000 clams in a single meal and would ruin the oyster beds.

Headlines such as **Loch Plunged into Walrus War** soon appeared. The spoof fooled the Scottish National Heritage and the Loch Fyne Marine Trust, both of whom wrote deeply serious columns on the danger of Walruses to oysters and other marine species. After a stunt like this, recognition of the Loch Fyne Oysters brand climbed up the scale. By this time, Loch Fyne Oysters had ceased to be just a supplier of oysters and other shellfish to London restaurants.

The first move towards retailing Oysters and other treasures of the sea at Loch Fyne had begun innocently enough in 1980 when Daniel Sumsion, a schoolboy nephew of Johnny, had begun to sell a variety of fish out of a fish box. From quite early on, Johnny and Andy had seen the logic of broadening the variety of fish and shellfish on sale to the wholesalers and London restaurateurs. Gordon Craig, for instance, a fisherman who owned a prawn boat, was in the habit of landing fresh langoustine at Crinan pier. Mussels were being harvested up the coast while Loch Fyne Oysters itself caught lobsters and crabs, while they bought in wonderful scallops gathered by divers in the loch.

Children brandishing sharp knives opened the oysters as orders arrived, working very short shifts. But clearly adults were needed to keep the place safe. Women from the village at Cairndow came to help meet the

demand from passing motorists. Andy Lane and David Weir, that first employee, joined in. It was so successful that Andy decided a hut should be put up to serve as a proper shop. From this, eventually, emerged the Loch Fyne Oyster Bar; a fine low building with its own car park and plenty of seats inside.

More people were now employed to man the shop and the bar. They proved very successful at giving every shopper or dining client a sense that they were something special. The shop soon had a turnover of £ 1million a year.

The foundations of a new restaurant chain that would send fish to all corners of Britain were being laid. People sometimes asked Andy Lane how he'd planned for all this. The truth was there was no strategic plan. "We just grew up to meet the demand," he assured me.

There is certainly a lot of truth in all that. But as the business grew it was clear that a large restaurant business required different talents from those of a simple start-up. The ambition to found a chain of shops and restaurants was there from an early age. The first attempt to get it right was in 1983 when a restaurant and shop was opened in William Street, Edinburgh, not far from the office of the European Union. But it failed to take off, demanding huge amounts of management time. Even ensuring a flow of fresh products every morning, delivered by van, was a nightmare.

The next two restaurants did not appear until years later. One was sited in Nottingham and the other at Elton near Peterborough. Both were close enough to the home of Martin Lane, Andy's brother, who helped fit them out.

By then, both Johnny and Andy appreciated that it took a quite different set of skills to run a chain of restaurants. They appointed head hunters to find the right person. In the end they found two, Ian Glyn and Mark Derry.

Ian had experience in finding profitable sites for restaurants. When interviewed for the job, Johnny and Mark were very impressed. They liked him, felt he could be trusted, and felt he would be quick to blend in with the distinctive culture found at Loch Fyne Oysters. Mark was willing to plough his own capital into the new firm that would build

and run the restaurant chain. In the end all four put in £250,000 each. It proved a good investment as the chain grew rapidly, investing profits into expansion.

Johnny never lived to see the dream completed but he would have been very happy with the outcome. In 2002, the year he died, ten restaurants were up-and-running. That number was to rise to 38 in 2007 and to 44 in 2009. Despite the great recession the firm has continued to thrive.

By the time Johnny died he presided over a growing and broadening empire that exported oysters to markets all over the world and had opened smokeries in Loch Fyne to supply its delicately smoked salmon and trout, as well as a mail order business. His new business employed well over a hundred people bringing employment to an unemployment black spot.

Looking back on the story, it is clear that Johnny, despite his eccentricities and the love of a good drink, was an inspiring leader whose faith in the people of Cairndow was amply rewarded.

He was a master of PR and publicity, becoming a flamboyant travelling advertisement for Loch Fyne Oysters. And he proved a great asset in extracting funds from his rich friends when they were needed. To the general public he was Loch Fyne Oysters. But he could never have succeeded without Andy Lane being at his elbow. Johnny admitted he was no good with figures and was by nature a chaotic individual. Entrepreneurs come in all shapes and sizes.

I last saw Johnny Noble in 2000 just two years before he died. The business had done so well that his 60 percent stake was now worth enough to pay off the family debts. His death was a blow, since no-one in the business had anything like his charisma and range of contacts. But the business was now mature enough to withstand his death and for it to emerge as a shining example of a worker-owned industry. This was very much down to Andy Lane and his determination that the business should not be taken over by strangers who were not steeped in the company's quite unique culture. With the help of the Baxi Partnership, a specialist in employee ownership, the company was restructured with Johnny Noble's shares committed in perpetuity to be the controlling interest. The remainder of

the shares could be bought by the workforce, but with no one allowed to own more than five percent of the employee shares.

Now in 2012 we can stand back and see how the company is doing. In 2002 the annual turnover was £7million. In 2012 that has risen to £22million. As for the workforce, this has grown to 105 staff. In February 2012 Loch Fyne Oysters received an investment boost from Scottish Seafood Investments which will allow it to capitalise on its brand and penetrate new export markets. Bruce Davidson, Managing Director of Loch Fyne Oysters heralded the move as "a new chapter in the company's history which will see the business move to the next level."

Looking back on Johnny Noble's adventures with the oysters, where does it fit into our search for that elusive **entrecode**®?

Noble had many of the characteristics of the good entrepreneur. I was particularly impressed by his stress on economy and on the need to conserve resources when you set out on the entrepreneur's path. When we discussed how this principle should be defined by entrepreneurs they had a phrase for it: 'roughing it at the start'.

In Johnny's case this was extended by a policy of 'beg, borrow and befriend', another catchy way of suggesting how resources can be conserved at the start-up stage. The twelve companies I researched all showed cautious prudence when it came to spending money. There was no sign of the entrepreneur as the Flash Harry, the barrow boy beloved by the media, swanning about in fast cars. Instead there was a quiet resourcefulness and a determined focus on the job in hand. They were heroes not spivs.

The other strength displayed by Johnny was his sudden flashes of brilliance, such as the decision to dispatch Andy to France. What would I have done in the situation the Bretons found themselves in? I hate saying it, but I think I would have run a mile. Competitive advantage is not easily gained and can be thrown away all too easily.

What did we learn from the Johnny Noble story?

You may have assets which could be turned into an opportunity by some creative thinking.

Look around the world and ask who does this well? You do not have to rediscover the wheel. You can build on other people's experiences and reduce the risk to your business.

Once you have a good product with an established name it may be possible to leverage it into other opportunities.

It is possible to get PR and marketing done on the cheap – if you are smart enough.

From Opportunity to Superior Opportunity

As Johnny Noble illustrates well, entrepreneurs spot opportunities to create valued businesses by marshalling the resources and then building the capability of their businesses to grow and expand. In Noble's case the opportunity was generated by finding himself facing a crisis in his own family a problem that needed to be solved. He resolved the problem by finding a gap in the market and filling this with a product that was very saleable. Properly marketed, and dedicated to delighting his customers, it was a winner.

But new entrepreneurs find that spotting an opportunity is not enough to guarantee growth and long-term success. Many small businesses are based on the corner shop concept. They see an opportunity and move in, only to find that there are already hundreds of companies in that crowded market place. They end up with a 'me-too' opportunity. The market is too crowded and everyone ends up cutting prices to the bone and working all hours, day and night. A new business might survive in such a market but it will never be able to charge the higher prices that open the way to business growth. For that you need a superior opportunity, one that offers a product or a service that is unique and not easily copied.

What is a Superior Opportunity?

Our research both with the Hallmarks companies and the Scottish growth businesses shows that it is one that:

Solves a real customer problem for which they are prepared to pay.

The product(s) or service(s) has a competitive advantage that can be defended, i.e. competitors cannot easily copy.

It is new, novel and original.

It attracts investors and media interest.

It has real growth potential.

Most opportunities do not meet these tough criteria but when they do, it's fantastic!

How can an entrepreneur find the superior opportunity?

Ann Adlington, Roger McKechnie, and Messrs.' Noble and Lane all discovered the secret, almost by accident, through following their instincts. Most great entrepreneurs have an unexpressed set of rules to guide their business by their entrepreneurial code. If we can unlock that code and make it universal in its appeal, we will be well on the way to opening the gateway to the flood of business ideas and business practices that can reshape the world.

People often ask if there is any one set of qualities that makes for success as an entrepreneur. While there are ways of making your fortune there are undoubtedly uncanny similarities in the methods used to establish a new company, especially one that will grow, provide much needed jobs, and make a personal fortune. That's why it is so useful to compare entrepreneurs from quite different social backgrounds. Let us turn to the astonishing story of how Sir Tom Hunter rose to become the richest man in Scotland in just 20 years.

While Johnny Noble came from a privileged background – he was educated at Eton – Tom Hunter grew up in the small mining village of New Cumnock in Ayrshire, 40 miles south of Glasgow. He was born in 1961; just ten years after a great pit disaster had reminded the village of the human costs of working underground in unstable land. A great influx of liquid peat had burst into the underground chambers and trapped over 100 men – after a 48-hour rescue operation most of them escaped with their lives though an unlucky 13 could not be saved. The tragedy scarred the village, but production was resumed and continued for another 20 years.

The Hunters had been in New Cumnock for generations running the local shop. But as Tom grew up it must have been clear it was serving

a declining community. Although he attended the well-respected Cumnock Academy he found school difficult, perhaps because he suffered from mild dyslexia'. He left school in 1977 and worked for a time in the family store before finding a place at Strathclyde University, studying marketing. When he graduated in 1981 he found there were no jobs on offer. He applied for over 200 vacancies and was granted only three interviews, all fruitless; he often notes he was 'unemployable'.

Even then there was an entrepreneurial streak in his character. As a youngster he had run his own video hire company out of his father's shop. Then, after graduation he took a place in a Glasgow University scheme for young businessmen and worked for a while on the *Glasgow Times*. While there, he worked out a plan to make it a free newspaper funded by advertising. He made an offer to the owner, Sir Hugh Fraser, who did not appreciate a cheeky 22-year-old advising him on how to run his paper. Frustrated, Whilst at University Tom had helped his father at weekends, who had sold up the store and taken a stake in a market stall in the coastal town of Irvine, selling shoes. It was here that he spotted his first 'superior opportunity'.

Young lads fresh from school came browsing through the stalls at the weekend looking for trendy gear. The big prize was to find a pair of trainers – shoes originally conceived as sportswear but now becoming the height of teenage fashion. Tom soon got fed up turning disappointed youths away.

As his father drove him home that night I imagine that Tom floated an idea, born of his encounter with these young people. What if he acquired a van and a travelling stall that he could take around the country? What if he were to win a 'concession'? Campbell Hunter may have been more than a little sceptical but he agreed to put up £5,000, while the Royal Bank of Scotland did the same. It meant Tom had just £10,000 to acquire the stock he would need and the all-important van.

He fired off a score of letters to every big retailer in the country on headed notepaper, boldly branded as SUPER SHOE and was now ready to start the search for his first customers. Within days he had received his first enquiry, from Peter Stores, who had branches across the north of England.

They wrote back to say they would grant him a 'concession' with one proviso – he had to have it up and running in just one week's time.

Tom began a frantic life, driving the van with the stocks up and down the country, sleeping in it when necessary and always carrying a neatly ironed shirt and suit to make the shop visits.

It was the beginning of a great success story. Soon he had opened concessions in Burtons, Fosters and a group called Concept Man, soon to be River Island. In 1989, at the age of 29, he opened the first of his own shops, Sports Division, in Paisley. In 1994 Tom told me he was good at doing deals with suppliers and motivating the sales teams. He hated running meetings and doing the formal management stuff. What should he do? I suggested he stick to what he was good at and get other people around him to do the things he was not good at and did not relish. I met Tom again in 2002 and he told me that he did exactly what I had suggested and that it was the best advice he had ever received. This is another example of building a team of people with complementary skills.

By 1995 his group had a turnover of £36 million and employed a staff of 1000. Shortly afterwards he took over the much larger Olympus chain of sports goods and fashion shops, giving him ownership of over 200 shops spread across the country. In 1998 JB Sports – run by Dave Whelan – offered £290 million for the Sports Division chain which Tom accepted, giving him a personal fortune worth £260million.

By this time he seemed unstoppable. He put money into a private equity company called West Coast Capital and a goodly sum into property investments and established, with his wife Marion, his own charitable foundation, The Hunter Foundation Through that he put up funds to help Scotland develop a more successful entrepreneurial community and enterprising educational system. In July 2005 he was knighted for his services to entrepreneurship and philanthropy. He and his wife have donated large sums to help young people in Scotland 'be all they can be'; for he had been inspired by Andrew Carnegie, the poor Scottish immigrant to the USA, who made a fortune in steel, and proceeded to give it all away. Carnegie has become something of a model for Tom to follow.

Unfortunately the great crash of 2008 led to the loss of a significant portion of his wealth. But for would-be entrepreneurs Tom Hunter's greatest service has been to demonstrate that great fortunes can be made even when the initial resources are scant and the road ahead has its bumpy passages. Some of those on the trail may have to go back and start again.

We had learned many lessons on our travels around Scotland and gained some valuable new insights into the behaviours of successful entrepreneurs. We knew what they did; spotting superior opportunities, serve an apprenticeship, build a team of people with complementary skills, for example, but we still had not discovered how they did it. If we were truly to crack the entrepreneurial code we needed to delve deeper into the mind of the entrepreneur. I was stuck with a dilemma for several years – would I ever find the answer and crack the entrepreneurial code?

These are the lessons of the Tom Hunter journey to wealth that illustrate some of the key lessons we discovered in our research with Scottish entrepreneurs.

Lessons Learned

- You don't need to come from a wealthy background to start a successful business.
- Try to find a superior opportunity not just a 'me-too' offer.
- Serve an apprenticeship in the type of business you want to – start to learn the ropes and spot superior opportunities at the same time.
- Find low-cost ways to start your business.
- Stick to what you are good at but get people around you who cover your weaknesses as you grow.
- Plan when to exit your business.

Chapter Six
Gadgets, Time Stretchers and Opening up the Mind

The three Scottish pioneers shared many of the marks of the classic entrepreneur. None of them shone at school, all three had created a superior opportunity that came from spotting a gap in the market and exploiting it before potential competitors had become alive to the possibilities. But there was something else that established companies lacked – the drive and determination that arose out of fulfilling a personal dream.

Having embarked on the course, their dedication and persistence saw them through to a triumphal conclusion. Still I would be misleading you to say that all start-up businesses sailed through the early days unscathed. My next port of call was 250 miles away on the banks of the Humber, in the worthy old city of Kingston Upon Hull – Hull to you and me.

I'd come to catch up on the heroic adventures of a self-made entrepreneur called Jonathan Elvidge. Jonathan, now 49 years old, became famous in the business community in the 1990s when he threw up his job working for the local telephone company, which involved climbing up poles, to set up his own business. For years Jonathan had dreamed of opening up a shop where he could get all his Christmas presents in one go. In 1990, Jonathan decided to turn his vision into reality and left to try his hand as an entrepreneur. There was no history of this in his family. What inspired him to throw caution to the wind was his love of gadgetry – he was a total fan of the Chinese-made gadgets that no man of a certain age would want to be without. As a businessman, he had a role model, albeit a negative role model, in the 1970s TV character Reggie Perrin, a nightmare landlord and indifferent shopkeeper. *The Grot Shop* he so mismanaged was the worst kind of shop possible – a rag and bone

concoction that sold goods of every kind to 'people with no taste'. The combination of the two worked on Jonathan's mind. He asked himself what the direct opposite of that kind of shop would be like. That became the model or his first venture into retail, a gleaming modern shop with everything neatly displayed and a place for every conceivable kind of present, provided they had some link with gadgetry.

Of course it cost money to fit out the shop just as he wanted it and to stock it up for the Christmas rush. But he had just remortgaged his house and put the money in the bank to run his business. With this he created a magical shop that he cleverly marketed as a 'one-stop-shop for presents'. It was the answer to the lazy man's dream. The customer could wait until the last minute on Christmas Eve or birthdays then call into the shop to solve his present-buying problems in a matter of minutes. News of this unique shop spread across Hull and the surrounding centres. That first Christmas it completely sold out the stock. This was achieved without a proper salesforce. There were three of them – himself, a friend, and the babysitter – enthusiastic volunteers, naïve but keen. Somehow they survived the rush.

Being an inexperienced entrepreneur with nothing but his own vision to guide him, he seemed to defy many of the conventions of high-value sales technique. Jonathan set the gifts up in see-through glass cases that were locked. A seasoned retailer warned him that this wouldn't work. Customers wanted to handle the goods and get the feel of them. Jonathan declined to change his visionary shop. In the end customers rather liked his approach.

He does admit to one major blunder. When he asked how much the rent for the shop was to be he was told it was £30,000 a year. He agreed to the deal. It was only later he discovered all the other shops (identical in size to his) paid much less. "Why did you not tell me there was a reduced rate?" he asked the manager, Andy Hobbs. "Because you never asked," came the reply. It was not the answer he wanted to hear. He had been working 60 hours a week to keep his head above water. Jonathan put it down to his naiveté and promised he would never again be a pushover. After this, however, things went more smoothly. When a survey was done

of the shopping centre, which included Marks and Spencer and Tesco, Jonathan's proved to have the third biggest turnover. Not bad for a naïve beginner.

By the summer of 1992 Jonathan ambitiously wanted to open two further shops. But he didn't have the capital needed. In the middle of the 90s recession the banks wouldn't lend the money. Andy Hobbs, who managed the shop complex, housing the first store, came to the rescue by offering to put in £25,000 for a 50 percent share of the business, he also got 50 percent of all future stores. The deal was agreed and there followed 10 very successful years.

It was helped by the fact that Andy Hobbs had experience of managing shops, leaving Jonathan to concentrate on buying the popular gadgets in the Far East. By the year 2000 the business had 45 stores and was valued at £50 million. It sounds like a fairy story – it was, but a fairy with power to make mischief. By the year 2000 Jonathan had ambitious plans to open more stores. This time (with Andy Hobb's agreement) Jonathan reinvested the profits from his business in order to open more stores – a smart move.

"I had arrived" Jonathan told me. "That was until Christmas 2001 when my world collapsed . We had an overdraft with the Nat West Bank of £4m which was needed each Christmas because that was when 50 percent of our sales was achieved." So he paid suppliers in November and filled the cash tills in the Christmas rush. Unfortunately, in 2001 the rush was less than he had previously experienced so he rang the bank from the Christmas party and asked them for a two- or three-week extension to his overdraft. The bank rang back hours later and cut his overdraft from £4m to £400K – he was sunk. "We were profitable, number one on the internet, but competition was creeping up on us and I had not seen it. The bank thought we were in trouble even though we were cash positive at the time." What could he do? Jonathan had to find money quickly. So he went to private equity providers and they drove a pretty hard bargain. "They would pump in £1 million in return for 90 percent of the business. I would be left with ten percent of the shares. But things got rapidly worse. The whole deal unravelled in the most horrific manner. The partners in

the equity fund fell to squabbling about who owned what."

The whole sad affair ended in a bitter high court dispute over ownership and on the 15th March 2005 The Gadget Shop went into receivership. The rights to the catchy name were bought up by W H Smith, Jonathan lost all the value of his remaining shares, while 800 staff lost their jobs. It was a bitter pill to swallow. So how did he feel? Does he regret it? "Well of course…but I met my new wife as a result and that's been great."

The story has a hard sweetness, but it does not end here. Jonathan had a dogged streak. He set about building a new business, called Red5, which now has a chain of eight stores across Britain and is expanding rapidly.

Jonathan's tale is a remarkable one. Although in the end he has survived and prospered, the last 15 years of his life have been troubled ones. I can't help thinking that Jonathan suffered from the limitations of being an entrepreneur with no previous experience. It underlines the need for a tight grasp on all the finance issues that may arise and also for the need for a much better networking between entrepreneurs with common interests and with something of mutual value to exchange.

Out of the debacle of the Gadget Shop affair, I was more than ever convinced that we had to find some way to provide the advice and support any entrepreneur needs at some time in their career. My first step was to gather together 30 Yorkshire entrepreneurs to see whether we could break down the barriers that tend to develop between them as the business matures and grows. It was at this session in 2002 that I became most aware of the problem we had yet to resolve. Putting it plainly, entrepreneurs seemed to have a completely different – at times infuriatingly different – ways of communicating compared with more ordinary mortals.

Think back a moment to the case of Jonathan Elvidge. How many of us would have done what he did by picking up the pieces and rebuilding his business from scratch? In an incredibly short time he had recreated the businesses, chosen the name of Red5, and got himself back on track. Yet when I asked him to explain how he managed this feat, step by step, he replied: "I dunno. I just did it." In fact it has become a catchphrase

among entrepreneurs. How do we explain it? There is an explanation, which you will see, but first let me show you the events that led up to the discovery of the invisible barrier that stands between entrepreneurs and those who work with them or try to train them, the 'entrepreneurial code'.

The first inkling I received of the deep-seated problem represented by the code came when I met up with the 30 entrepreneurs to seek a way forward. The first of what was to become a series of support sessions took place in January 2002. The agenda? *Promoting better networking in the entrepreneurial world.* The meeting was held under the auspices of the local support agency, South Yorkshire Business Link at a local hotel in Sheffield.

I led the discussion. We wanted to measure just how effective the present informal links were in spreading good practice among entrepreneurs. I lined up a few of our best entrepreneurs to explain how they worked. They were surprisingly tongue-tied.

Networking was defined in my book *In the Company of Heroes* as 'building strong personal and working relationships with people who can help build your business.' The definition suffers from being a little vague. What constitutes a strong personal and working relationship? One entrepreneur based in Glasgow once confided in me about the use he made of the local business club.

"When I first started I attended every breakfast, lunch and dinner meeting I possibly could, to try and build up useful contacts. I didn't create one jot of business but I did put on two stone. I learnt the hard way that you need to pick and choose who you network with. I now only network very selectively."

Yet the truth is that networking – conducted properly – can make a huge difference to a business. Research has shown it to be a key business building skill. It has been shown to be the strongest predictor of long-term success.

At the meeting I tried to get the entrepreneurs and their support staff to experiment to try out ways of working that would lead to greater collaboration between them. The discussion led us to consider a device that had been tried out in small groups but never tested before on a significant scale. This is how it worked:

The 30 people were arranged in a circle of 15 tables with two people seated at each table. Each had a large A3 display pad. We called the game Needs and Offers. Each person wrote their three most important business needs on one sheet of paper and three ideas they could offer in exchange on another. They spent ten minutes chatting about the needs and offers and then moved to the next table if on the outside of the ring – staying where they were if on the inside. The idea created a great deal of interest, quite a stir, since it got the entrepreneurs and their business supporters talking in practical terms and helping each other by matching needs and offers. At the end of the session there was a chance for each participant to make a deal on an exchange basis. Quite a few very sound business ideas arose out of this one session. It has been repeated since with great success.

One of the key lessons we learned from this exercise and further research was how entrepreneurs prefer to learn.

Entrepreneurial Learning	Traditional Business Support
Just doing it	From successful peers
Family and friends	Training courses
Text books	'Experts' and consultants

No wonder less than 7% of the entrepreneurs we researched sought or valued support from the traditional business support offerings!

Lesson for the business support network:

Offer support in the ways entrepreneur's value and they will work with you.

But one interesting insight into the entrepreneurial mind showed itself on that first day. If you asked one of them to tell us how they had come to produce a particularly successful idea, time and time again, they could not explain the train of thought that gave rise to it. There was no hint of an analytical process, or even the use of deduction. It was a genuine puzzle that I only got to grips with three years ago. It concerned the

difference between rational people and creative people. There have been lots of books published recently that deal with the inexplicable qualities of the human mind (see for example Malcolm Gladwell's *Blink – the power of thinking without thinking*). It occurred to me way back in 2002 that entrepreneurs seemed to possess the ability to think without thinking. Now it seemed worth exploring in depth, but where could I start?

Luck intervened. One morning I was visiting the Business Link South Yorkshire and happened to bump into Anne Selwyn, a local business advisor who I had worked with, on and off, for nearly five years. Over coffee, I talked about my thoughts on the entrepreneurial brain. She became quite animated and suggested I'd find the answer in America. She had just returned from Denmark where she had been on a course run by Wyatt-Woodsmall, a course which touched on new discoveries about how the creative brain works.

I asked Anne if he was a business consultant. "Not really," she replied, "he specialises in sports people and in the military top brass. Quite a fascinating man. One of his greatest admirers is the Olympic high board diver, Greg Louganis. He helped him win three gold medals at the Olympic Games." It intrigued me that one man could have spread his net so widely. According to Anne he was a world leader in the new science of high performance and had already shown that a diver could mentally stretch the time available for action between the starting signal and take-off by a factor of four. This accounted for Greg Louganis' astonishing performances in the Olympic pool.

When I got home that night I put a call through to Wyatt-Woodsmall and told him of my search for an explanation of the entrepreneurial inability to explain things logically. Despite our different backgrounds we immediately struck up a rapport. I booked a flight to Washington for the very next day.

He turned out to be an interesting guy, an ex- park ranger in Yellowstone National Park who possessed the largest set of eyebrows I had ever seen. Wyatt lived just outside Washington on a posh housing estate. It was a massive house, filled with old American antiques, statues of Budda and candles. There was a whiff of hippiness about it, a bit New Age. He had

several white cats which I found unsettling. At the back of the house there was a double office, one for him and one for his wife Marilyne, laid out and decorated in the same way – his and hers, all matching chairs, computers and equipment. All rather curious.... In later life he had taken a degree in psychology and had become nationally famous – among sports fans at least – when he worked with Greg Louganis, America's gifted highboard and springboard diver. Louganis became the first man to win consecutive Olympic gold medals (1984 and 1998) in the platform and springboard events, a feat unequalled to this day. He achieved his springboard victory at the Seoul Games in 1988 despite striking the board with his head.

I peppered Wyatt with questions over a light lunch. He had been hired by the USA Olympic coaches to work out how Louganis scored his perfect tens in order to pass on his secret to other members of the team. Wyatt took up the story: "I first met Greg at a Thai Restaurant. He ordered a curry and the waitress asked how spicy he wanted it on a scale of one to ten. "Ten," he replied. Taken aback, the waitress asked him if he'd tried a ten before. When his meal came Louganis finished it without breaking sweat.

I asked Greg how he got perfect tens and his reply was "I don't know, I just do it." So we filmed him diving. We interviewed him several times, photographed him and studied hundreds of pictures but we could not fathom out how he did it.

"Then one day I said to him, "Greg, even when you do not get off the board 100 percent correct you still seem to correct your dive in the 2.6 seconds it takes to hit the water. How do you do that?"

Greg looked surprised. "2.6 seconds? No, I have about 10 seconds." Wyatt had interrupted him at this point.

"But Greg, we've timed you with stopwatches – it's 2.6 seconds not 10, how can that be?"

"Ah," Greg replied, "well when I get to the end of the board I have taught myself to meditate quickly so that when I go off the board in my mind I have enough time to get the dive right. I thought everybody knew that."

It was an odd concept. But it seemed to make perfect sense to the diver. Wyatt had winkled another even more startling revelation out of the diver by asking, "Do you do anything else to get perfect dives that you forgot to tell me?"

"Well yes, in the dressing room when I am waiting for a dive I watch myself on a small video doing perfect dives over and over again. So when I get on the board and slow my mind down my presumably unconscious brain takes over and I produce the perfect dive."

"That's it?" Wyatt blurted out amazed.

"Yes, that's it," confirmed Greg. "I just do it."

I quizzed Wyatt about whether his approach could help me in my search for an understanding of why entrepreneurs in general failed miserably when it came to explaining just why they decided to take one course of action rather than another. He suggested it might be explained by the fact that entrepreneurs didn't think the way most people did. By that he meant that they assumed everybody thought like them. In working with servicemen he had come across many people who thought intuitively and made no allowance for other modes of thought. They had a state of mind that he had dubbed 'unconsciously competent'. It was entirely possible to coach people to tackle the problem. In fact he had run something similar, for the US Army.

I was sold on the idea. He agreed to come to Yorkshire to carry out a study of the entrepreneurs in action if I could raise the money to pay for it. It would not come cheap. The price tag was £100,000. So convinced was I that Wyatt could deliver what he promised, I agreed the deal. On the understanding that the money would be there, he agreed to come to Yorkshire to carry out his assessment and work with me to produce a research paper on how to turn Yorkshire's small businesses into world beaters. I flew back to London a happy man.

Lessons Learned

- Some opportunities can be created by resolving a problem that you as an individual are passionate about.

- Be careful about the partners you take on, particularly where there is finance involved.

- Being able to recover from setbacks is a key entrepreneurial trait.

- Entrepreneurs prefer to learn from their peers rather than from experts or consultants.

- There is an answer to every problem providing you are persistent in looking for them.

Chapter Seven
The Code is Cracked

It's late afternoon and I wait impatiently at Doncaster station for the arrival of the London train. Wyatt Woodsmall should be on it, but it's running late.

A visit to America to meet Wyatt was to prove a turning point in my quest to crack the Entrepreneurial Code. My work on the *Hallmarks* research between 1990 and 1992 had started the quest. That slim volume had destroyed the myths that entrepreneurs could be successful if given a course in financial or business management. Entrepreneurs behaved quite differently from those working in long-established and larger firms. But this fact had not yet had any impact on the powers that be in most governments around the world, who had stubbornly stuck with the belief that teaching entrepreneurs how to write a business plan would ensure their success.

The BBC asked me to turn my *Hallmarks* work into a six-part series for television, and I was extremely proud when it won a BAFTA at the Royal Television Society Awards.

The *Hallmarks* research was followed by a book that revealed entrepreneurs had often followed a common path on their road to enlightenment. *In the Company of Heroes* found that many successful entrepreneurs had served a form of informal apprenticeship. They were often people who had grown tired of working for a large enterprise and the bureaucracy that so often went with it.

Far from being wealthy individuals, most entrepreneurs came from modest backgrounds. They often got started on the kitchen table or, in

the case of Tom Hunter, by living and working in a far from comfortable van. The ones I worked with even invented their own catchphrases to describe what they did – roughing it from the start to conserve cash, backfilling the business to keep it well managed as it stretched and grew, problem seeking/problem solving to bring in the customers and ensure they would come back.

In the Company of Heroes was intended to be a working handbook for entrepreneurs and an introduction to the subject for those considering taking the plunge. In both cases, it proved a great success because it set out **WHAT** entrepreneurs actually do to create success. However, it could scarcely have been the last word. There was a black hole at its centre – the mystery of tongue-tied entrepreneurs, which was **HOW** they created success. For example, we discovered that they networked to create opportunities, but HOW did they go about networking?

Of course, there is one good reason for entrepreneurs not to be unduly given to baring their soul and telling a casual visitor exactly how the business was doing, what plans they might have for launching new products or services and so on. They are operating in a competitive market and might be expected to remain tight-lipped about anything that could be regarded a trade secret. However, I had known many of the entrepreneurs for years and they trusted me. I had maintained a professional distance from them and was certainly not going to rush off and break confidences by revealing sensitive details to rival companies. As a result, I was welcomed by most entrepreneurs that I worked with as a useful sounding board and helper.

But when I asked an entrepreneur a question that should have been easy to answer (such as "What strategy did you adopt to win, say, that £500,000 contract for computer services?") the entrepreneur would typically reply, "I don't know. I don't think I had one. I just did what I had to do."

At the time I tended to think it was explained by reticence on the part of the entrepreneur, but when the pattern repeated itself with other entrepreneurs I came to the conclusion there was a disconnect between the mind of the entrepreneur and that of other "normal" people.

The frequency of entrepreneurs bringing the shutters down on any further discussion when I inquired HOW they had achieved this or that outcome made me despair of making any further progress in the task of understanding the way successful entrepreneurs worked. If I couldn't get round this problem I was stuck. This was the impasse that I came to see as a barrier. The entrepreneurs possessed a unique way of doing things, a code of operation that needed to be understood before I could proceed with my fourth and final book. That was what 'cracking the code' was all about.

It was the quest for the key to the entrepreneurial mind that led me to Wyatt Woodsmall in Washington DC. There, Wyatt had assured me that the mystery would be solved by the fresh insights into how the mind worked provided by the developing science of High Performance. To me, an amateur when it came to such things, this seemed a bit like smoke and mirrors, but I resolved to give it a try.

We raised sponsorship from the regional development agency and local Business Link. I myself matched the funding to enable us to bring Wyatt across from the States to work with a selection of 40 successful entrepreneurs. We carefully picked entrepreneurs who had been trading for 10 years and had a track record of growth in sales, profits and number of employees. We also selected people who were held up in their industry and region as role models and leaders. We then extended our sample of entrepreneurs to over 300 both in the UK and Australia. If you are interested in the details of the research process then this can be requested via my website *www.davidhalluk.com* **'Research findings in to the way entrepreneurs start and build high growth businesses.'**

On cue, the London train pulled into the station. Held at bay by a barrier, I watched as an enormous trunk was disgorged from the first class section, gingerly followed by Wyatt. It looked like he intended to stay for months, not just the six weeks we had agreed. But I was soon to learn that Wyatt was meticulously well-organised and had come prepared for any weather and for anything the interviews might throw up.

I shook his hand as he reached the exit barrier and greeted him warmly: "Welcome to Doncaster, the pride of Yorkshire." He didn't get the joke, but I packed the large case into the boot and drove him the ten miles to

my home. After an introduction to my wife, Ellen, I settled him into the guest bedroom (where in true American fashion he laid out a collection of health supplements). Half an hour later he came downstairs to share some steak and kidney pudding, washed down with a glass of the best Burgundy to be found.

The next morning we were up bright and early and, after a light breakfast, got down to the serious business of finding a way to crack the elusive code. In preparation for the task, we had arranged to meet some forty of the most successful entrepreneurs from Yorkshire and the surrounding counties. They had not been chosen at random, but by having at least ten years' experience and solid financial accounts. We expected each of the businesses to have a reasonably good track record in terms of profits, sales and a growing number of employees.

Wyatt had explained the choice this way. He was looking for 'high performance' people since that was his speciality, and he had shown that many such people – whether in the armed forces, large corporations, or the field of athletics – had demonstrated they could be trained to attain seemingly impossible goals through the power of the mind. This was especially true of individuals with 'creative and innovative' minds, who displayed the intuitive mode of thinking I had encountered in many entrepreneurs. Although I was aware of this phenomenon, it was Wyatt who showed me that finding this sort of person and putting them through the rigours of high performance analysis offered the best hope of cracking the code.

That first morning I described the frustration I had felt when asking entrepreneurs why they had chosen a certain course of action over another, only to be told they could not explain it. Was there something missing in their make-up? In his gravelly American voice, Wyatt gave me his explanation. It was because they were **unconsciously competent**. That meant they might perform well in business, athletics or what have you without ever realising what valuable skills they possess or how they came to acquire them.

Wyatt went on to explain that unconscious competence makes it difficult for people to pass on the skills they have acquired over the years to

others. The result? A poorly performing company. The evidence for this is simply that successful entrepreneurs rarely develop other successful entrepreneurs because they can't tell them how to do it. The good news, he told me, is that it's possible to train people to become aware of these skills; that makes it possible for them to pass the skills on to others, increasing the possibility of success.

"Do you see what that means?" asked Wyatt. "The skills base in any country can be multiplied and multiplied again."

While Wyatt grew more excited with the very notion, I was left a little puzzled. Just what did this have to do with cracking the code? Wyatt spelt it out in that didactic manner I had become so used to. "Unconscious competence is something I would expect to find in huge quantities in new businesses. From what you've told me, most entrepreneurs left school early, presumably because they couldn't see the point of it. If they were lucky enough to be taken on by an employer they would learn on the job, which just happens to be the best way both to learn and to think in an intuitive way. If we could take these people and train them to be conscious of the skills they already possessed … Well. You see what I mean?"

I could see what he meant. But would eliminating unconscious competence really result in breaking the code that kept entrepreneurs and others apart? I was prepared to be convinced.

That morning we spent time putting the final touches to our plans for the research that would test Wyatt's theory to destruction. As well as recruiting 40 volunteer entrepreneurs – a task handled efficiently by the local Business Link service, a UK government agency – we had arranged to send a questionnaire to 250 other small or smallish businesses in the north of England and to forty firms in the City of Perth in Western Australia, where I had a good contact in Tim Atterton, a former Director of the Durham University Small Business Centre. The questionnaire covered the same ground as the in-depth interviews, and was designed to identify the key factors that strongly correlated with successful business performance over time.

At Wyatt's request, the two of us began by interviewing one of the most promising of the forty local entrepreneurs, whose business was based less

than ten miles away. It was agreed in advance that the interviews were to be conducted on a strictly confidential basis, with the entrepreneur guaranteed anonymity, in the hope this would encourage honest and open replies.

I kicked off by introducing Wyatt and outlining the nature of the research programme. I already detected a certain air of *ennui*, since entrepreneurs do not generally make good listeners. But when I asked him to tell us about his business, how it got started, what difficulties he had encountered and so on, his face lit up and his body language changed dramatically. So did Wyatt's. For the next twenty minutes, our interviewee unburdened himself while Wyatt madly scribbled notes. Our entrepreneur had been transformed from a dull and outwardly slightly depressed individual into one of the heroes I had written about in my second book.

Wyatt now took his turn and asked this newly emerged hero if he had ever heard the term 'in the zone'. "Well, I've heard of it in relation to golf," he told us. "Don't top golfers use that sort of approach? Getting the mind ready for the challenge." "Yes," said Wyatt, "but what do you think of applying it to your business?" He confessed he had never given it a thought. "But are you a change person or a keep-it-as-it-is person?" There was no doubt whose side he was on: "I welcome change," he said "with open arms."

This guy was flying, and clearly excited by the line Wyatt was taking. Throughout this open two-way discussion I had been taking notes, as had Wyatt. But his were quite different in quantity and purpose to mine, and when the three-hour interview came to an end Wyatt and I had a quiet lunch and headed back to base.

Had it gone well? I wondered. I asked Wyatt if he was happy with the discussion about getting into the zone. He was delighted that the entrepreneur had been so open-minded about looking at the world from a different perspective. However, it was what he had expected of someone who was clearly in the high performance category that Wyatt had identified as the most fruitful territory in which to suggest new ideas.

Getting In The Zone

The idea of 'the zone' is established, but mainly as a mental refuge where top athletes can prepare themselves for action in a big event. It involves breathing exercises and a focus on the body and mind (almost a state of self-hypnosis) designed to prepare the athletes for the challenge that lies ahead.

Once in the comfort of the dining room back home we began to review what we had achieved. I was curious about the reams of notes Wyatt had copied out during the session, particularly in relation to the zone. What was the point when we had a tape recording of the entire discussion? Wyatt raised his formidable eyebrows. "You've a lot to learn," he said.

He explained that verbal language was over-rated as a medium of communication. In any oral interaction, only ten per cent of the information came from the spoken word. That compared to the twenty per cent that came from intonation – the tone of voice – and the remaining seventy per cent communicated by body language. That was why he had gazed so intently at the entrepreneur during the long interview, noting the expression in the eyes, the little tell-tale mannerisms that told him about the state of mind and just what emotions were present. We spent hours listening to the tapes, annotating the perceived strengths and weaknesses of this first entrepreneur. We then went over the accounts of our next entrepreneur and by ten o'clock had gone to bed, ready for another strenuous day.

This is the pattern we repeated over the following months, broken only by a return to Washington to work with Marilyne Woodsmall on the entrepreneur tapes.

Marilyne, who describes herself as a mind coach, is an advisor to companies and individuals on how to improve their performance using the insights that come from high performance. One special skill she possesses is the ability to analyse taped conversations and extract special factors that have a bearing on the performance of the company, giving due weight to the evidence presented by the entrepreneur.

To give you an example, Marilyne can judge just how focused the entrepreneur is on the business when it really matters, say in their approach to securing a major new contract – information that could be deduced from the tapes, the accounts and the body language detected by Wyatt. How do they stay focused? We discovered that they keep their eyes on the prize, as one entrepreneur described his process. They work out the result they want and then allow their minds to concentrate on what is required to achieve it. "Everything else is a distraction" was how many described their disciplined approach to focusing on the key issues.

"It's obvious," one entrepreneur said, "if I find a customer problem which is causing them real pain and I solve it for them then that's not selling like everybody else and the price is usually irrelevant. Finding and solving customer problems has created competitive advantage in most of our customers." I will discuss problem seeking in more detail later.

Focus and problem seeking were just two of the many skills that might ultimately determine the success or failure of the company. After that first spell in Washington DC, such details were listed as 'factors' that could decide the future of the company. At one point in the process we had identified no less than 96 of these factors that clearly related to performance.

In trying to design an ideal mix of the qualities needed to maximise the chances of success and keeping the package simple, we decided that 96 was too big a number. After lengthy discussion and debate, we reduced the number of factors to just 21 by distributing a questionnaire to 300 entrepreneurs and correlating their responses with the performance of their businesses over time.

But that is to jump ahead. It was clear at this early stage that we would end up with a package of factors that would revolutionise thinking on how best to create an enduring and expanding business.

Obviously, it is impossible to give a full blow-by-blow account of everything we considered during the six weeks Wyatt spent with me. But if you take that first interview and multiply it by forty you'd get some feel for the intense workload we undertook. The urgent need was to find a

way to turn a tongue-tied entrepreneur into an articulate and charismatic leader of a team. I believed that based on what I had already seen – the animated, lit-up face and sparkling eyes of our first entrepreneur – the transformation was indeed possible.

In the weeks that followed we came across plenty of new evidence to justify that optimism. Take for instance the case of one of the better-known entrepreneurs, a man whose accounts and track record, on paper at least, suggested he would be worth speaking to. We drove twenty miles to meet him at his company HQ. I should explain we made a point of visiting the entrepreneurs on their home territory, so to speak; it gave us a chance to have a look at the business firstly from the outside and then inside too. As was our custom, we made detailed notes.

This very successful start-up business (now ten years old) showed every sign of being a booming enterprise. The building looked custom built and at most only a few years old. There was a thoughtful sign welcoming visitors and indicating exactly where to find the visitors' entrance. You could see and smell the success of the business when you walked through the door. Inside, the reception was friendly and our interviewee, the lead entrepreneur, came out to meet us and show us into the office. We settled down with a cup of herbal tea while I introduced Wyatt and outlined what we had come to do.

This second entrepreneur, like the first, was predictably, in Wyatt's jargon, a high performer, with a very strong set of accounts and apparently surviving the recession in rude health. We started to discuss the business and the threats and opportunities it now faced. Wyatt took the lead, as he was anxious to explore where the energy so apparent in the body language of the staff came from.

"I think it's just a reflection of the fact that people genuinely like working here," he said.

"I think you're being unduly modest," Wyatt replied. "Don't you have some kind of grand vision that people can relate to?"

"Well, we have a mission and vision statement – that gives us something short and snappy."

Wyatt broke off from his note taking to make his point more forcefully. "I am not thinking of some sort of little plaque stuck up on the wall. I am thinking of something much bigger, more impactful. I am thinking of the personal vision you have for your company. If it is strong enough you will feel yourself taken over by this vision, and that in turn will energise you to be bold and think bigger." This was, he explained, something he called a 'compelling vision'.

The way we got to the idea of a compelling vision provides a useful insight into Wyatt's way of unlocking the code. He noticed that when an entrepreneur had done less well than they had hoped, their vision was often described in numbers, i.e. sales and profits. A bland vision led to a bland performance. With the entrepreneurs that had been very successful, we noticed that they came alive, they became animated, and as they described their vision it was as if they could see it as a video in vivid colour. Wyatt said, "They were so excited by their vision they actually licked their lips – they could see it, smell it and taste it and that's what turned them on!"

Every entrepreneur needs a compelling vision.

Compelling Vision

A picture of what the end game will look like which is highly motivating.

"There's only one thing," I added. "You have got to believe in it. If you only pretend to believe it, your body language will give you away."

Wyatt followed up with a pithy observation. "You see," he drawled, "all the research I have done in America has shown up vision as really important in creating the drive the company needed to go on to better things."

Our entrepreneur was fired up by now. He wanted to know more about vision and drive, and how Wyatt was so sure that the one led to the other.

"You only have to look at the exploits of Greg Louganis, the American Olympic diver I coached. He learnt to enter 'the zone' and carry his vision of the perfect dive with him. He reinforced that by playing a video

of one of his perfect dives over and over again. It worked for him. It will work for you too if you only try it."

The arrival of Wyatt on the scene was certainly making entrepreneurs think afresh. It was his passionate belief in development that made them see that thinking differently really paid off. Wyatt was keen to push ahead to address some of the biggest issues in the entrepreneurs' behaviour.

Our third entrepreneur opened up the possibility of boosting and releasing the drive that every entrepreneur worth his or her salt possesses. That drive is a key entrepreneurial process that is widely recognised among those who have started up their own businesses. But where does drive come from and how can it be boosted? Wyatt was convinced that drive was generated by negative experiences in early adulthood, and that a dash of positive experience might serve to strengthen it. This certainly corresponds with my own personal experiences, as we explored in Chapter Three. According to Wyatt, a taste of success following a dose of failure generates the real boost in drive.

How had our entrepreneurs faired at school? "Well, actually, I struggled because I was dyslexic and left school early with no qualifications, but I was determined to prove to myself and everybody else that I was OK," said our third entrepreneur.

In all the interviews we conducted, and in talking to entrepreneurs I have met since, something like forty per cent left school early with no qualifications, and around twenty per cent admitted to being dyslexic. Actually, to digress, it has been found that seventy per cent of people in prisons around the world are dyslexic.

Failure at school does not appear to hold entrepreneurs back. In fact, it seems to motivate them to succeed!

Our third entrepreneur sensed there was something in this theory. But he was more interested in how exactly he might boost the drive. Wyatt had an answer. It was a matter of turning away from failure to focus on a compelling vision of success – a mind thing. This is how he described it to us:

> ### Drive
>
> "This combination of moving away from failure towards achieving a dream provides the energy and rocket fuel in successful entrepreneurs.
>
> It also reminds us that success often comes out of adversity (earning it) as opposed to privilege (deserving it). Our research suggests that without this strong drive and need for achievement; entrepreneurs are unable to maintain the energy and commitment necessary to create a successful, high growth business."

This was all very well, but could the entrepreneur summon up the optimism that was deemed part and parcel of the process – especially in the aftermath of some setback that experience showed was hard for entrepreneurs to avoid?

As we travelled around the country this was a question that came up again and again. The path to ultimate success is a hard and rocky one, and nobody can guarantee that the setbacks encountered will be few and far between. What matters, Wyatt maintained, was the ability to recover from those that came along. As we conducted the survey we were anxious to discover the best strategies for entrepreneurs to adopt to make such a recovery speedy and as pain free as possible.

The more successful small and medium-sized firms regarded setbacks as the norm rather than the exception. It followed therefore that the company concerned needed to raise the motivation of all the staff to counter the setback. Having a compelling vision (which most of the better companies already had in some form or another) was a good starting point. It raised the adrenaline level and strengthened the will to fight back. The best firms backed this up by making sure all energy was focused on the immediate need to put matters right. If the problem arose through a fall in sales then efforts had to be concentrated on analysing why this was the case and taking remedial action, both in terms of retaining existing customers and bringing in new ones through problem seeking and problem solving.

It was obvious to me and Wyatt that companies that had recruited wisely and built a team ethos were much more likely to survive any setback than firms who had allowed things to slide and had lost all focus on priorities.

It is impossible in a single volume to do justice to the sheer volume of new material on small to medium-sized business that Wyatt and I gathered in our research project. In the pages that follow (Chapters 8 to 13) you will find much evidence to show just why some companies flourish and others don't.

One interesting finding was that entrepreneurs who defined their goal in purely monetary terms (for instance an ambition to make that first million pounds) came across as far less robust than those who expressed their goals in broader and more humanitarian terms. Thus, a company like Loch Fyne Oysters (not a part of this new study) prospered through some hard times because both directors and the staff saw themselves as creating local employment in a remote part of Scotland to help preserve a community.

This drove both Wyatt and I to think that people who run small to medium-sized businesses should redesign their mission statements to emphasise their commitment to a worthwhile cause. However, this would do little good – quite the opposite in fact – if the top management in their hearts couldn't care less.

By the time we finished the in-depth interviews a clear picture had emerged. The less successful entrepreneurs were ones that had never broken out of their limited vision of simply being their own boss. They were happy to soldier on, making some kind of living for themselves and often their family. What they did not possess was much interest in creating a firm that was going to expand to become a significant employer. Thirty years of government pressure to go out and think big had made little impact. They also showed little interest in trying out new ideas. The idea of a 'zone', into which the owner-manager could mentally retreat to prepare mind and soul for creating a growing company, simply didn't appeal.

The larger companies, on the other hand, seemed keen to discuss with Wyatt and myself how to shift the company into a new and higher gear.

While some remained sceptical about changing the company culture and the way of doing things, they were willing to give the new ideas a go, to be pleasantly surprised at the difference new thinking could make.

The best entrepreneurs displayed more than just a willingness to change. Over ten years all firms have their ups and downs, and survival and reinvention depend on one virtue above all else – persistence. When we asked about this it did not immediately strike a chord. One entrepreneur said he could not recall in practice being persistent. "Let's think for a minute," I said. "Have you ever had trouble funding the business?" I suggested (thinking of Jonathan Elvidge).

"Well, I did actually have an initial problem. I tried raising money from seventy-nine sources of finance. It was only on the eightieth attempt I finally convinced a venture capitalist I had the germ of a good idea."

That's persistence for you.

After four months of intensive research into how the forty entrepreneurs selected actually ran their businesses, Wyatt and I had laid the foundations of a new way to develop entrepreneurs both to increase their effectiveness and to open up the full potential of their businesses. The questionnaires issued to entrepreneurs in Britain and Australia stood the test, supporting the research's statistical significance.

Entrepreneurs are driven by a form of emotional intelligence. They learn by doing rather than from books or videos. They are easily bored and have a trait in their character that predisposes them to intuitive action. The educational system in Britain and most other countries does them no favours, biased as it is towards academic book learning. The development of entrepreneurs has been mishandled, because it was assumed that watered-down business books could simply be adapted for use by budding entrepreneurs.

After thirty-odd years of arguing for something more suited to creative thinkers and doers, I felt vindicated by the freedom to design and implement programmes based on our new insights into how entrepreneurial types work – as you will see below.

The one obvious difficulty facing anyone who wants to produce a workplace brimming with entrepreneurial skills is the awkward fact that, on the surface at least, entrepreneurs are born rather than bred. Wyatt and Marilyne believe that up to fifteen per cent of people are creative doers, and therefore likely to make successful entrepreneurs. But in most countries only about three per cent of people actually run a business employing more than three people, meaning there is plenty of room for increasing the flow of entrepreneurs into the small to medium-sized companies sector.

Wyatt argues that there is another way to swell the number of entrepreneurs. He thinks people can be trained to think and act in an entrepreneurial manner, which is clear from a plug used to sell his book:

The Science of Advanced Behavioral Modelling

Capture, Replicate and Transfer ANY Expertise, Ability or Skill rapidly and cost-effectively

Dr. Wyatt Woodsmall was instrumental in pioneering the concept and application of behavioural modelling technology while working on various projects for the U.S. Government. He has since developed several systems to improve the training processes and replicate expertise within an organization.

Once a high performance model is identified, it is possible to replicate and transfer the key factors of that high performance.

Through Advanced Behavioral Modelling SM training processes, any individual or organization can now replicate the skills and expertise of the world's best models of performance and install that top performance behaviour in themselves or throughout an entire organization.

Can it be done? It's certainly worth a try. Not all the American divers were creative people, yet they seemed to find it possible to all but match Greg Louganis's attainments using the zone and the video-in-the-head as effective tools. What is certainly true is that people can learn to

understand how they may differ. Having good entrepreneurs is a must if a business is to go on growing. It has certainly been for the best that Steve Jobs was not the only entrepreneurial spirit in the Apple business.

As business leaders, entrepreneurs have strengths and weaknesses; they may be brilliant at spotting opportunities but less good when it comes to other entrepreneurial skills, such as prioritising. Entrepreneurs often struggle to prioritise because they normally possess a low boredom threshold and move quickly between activities. In order to stay focused, and therefore successful, we discovered the most successful ones are good at maintaining goal-directed energy.

They decide on their long-term goal and then work back from that to the steps they need to take to achieve it. Once they settle on the first step, they work hard at not becoming distracted.

Spending four months researching how entrepreneurs built up their businesses was rich in revelation and in promoting a new understanding of how they actually created great businesses. In this chapter, I have shared just a few of the factors that contribute to entrepreneurial success.

However, another bonus came out of the blue when Professor Peter Saville, a world-renowned guru of talent management, approached me. He devises and provides personality tests to help companies recruit the most suitable candidates and individuals to maximise their chances of finding a rewarding career. He had heard about our research and wanted to produce a test to identify entrepreneurial talent. He found that our report on 'cracking the code' was well matched to the needs of clients. Ajaz Ahmed, the entrepreneur who did so much to make online shopping a reality in Britain, agreed to complete the test, and the results showed where his entrepreneurial strengths lay. For example, in 'Seeing Possibilities' (the ability to take in information and create insights), Ajaz notched up a score that placed him in the top one per cent of the population. In the test of his ability to network, 'Opening Up to the World', he was equally impressive, again placed in the top one per cent. He demonstrated both his passion and his ability to win people over to his cause, vitally important weapons in the entrepreneur's armoury (see *www.savilleconsulting.com*).

Peter Saville's test was the last piece of the jigsaw that prepared the way for the revolutionary breakthrough. For two years I had been working hard to produce a working model of the entrepreneur's code that would bring both entrepreneurs and their supporting team together. This had emerged as the **entrecode**®. The outline of the **entrecode**®, which has a modular structure and can be approached from many different angles, is laid out in Chapter 15. Any advisor, when properly certified to use the **entrecode**®, will find that it unlocks the barriers that have held back the dynamism of the start-up and growth businesses around the world.

Twenty years ago, I started out on my quest to crack the code and so release the potential of small to medium-sized companies, a power that can change the world and help us recover from the global recession. Eight years ago, with the help of Wyatt Woodsmall, I launched the **entrecode**®. Since then I have taken the message across continents and oceans, a simple message that spelt out the much under-rated value of the entrepreneur and the shameful lack of support to help those prepared to have a go at running a new business. My journey took me from all corners of Britain to France to Australia and then on to the USA.

Everywhere I went I was met by enthusiastic entrepreneurs anxious for some basic understanding and more sophisticated help to create a successful entrepreneurial business. Above all, two moments stand out because they made me feel passionately that I had been on the right track in believing I had cracked the code.

It was at a conference in San Francisco, attended by many of the best entrepreneurs in Silicon Valley. I delivered a keynote lecture on my investigation into the world entrepreneurs inhabit, their dreams and disappointments, their irrepressibility, their persistence, their remarkable powers of endurance in the face of adversity. At the end I received a standing ovation. One remark flew across the lecture theatre and carried above all the rest: "It's our life you have described!" That one note of appreciation made the years of endeavour in wrestling to uncover the secrets of entrepreneurial success all seem worthwhile.

I presented my **entrecode** findings to an entrepreneurial conference in Perth, Australia in 2004. Unbeknown to me, Professor Allan Gibb, the man

who challenged me to crack the code, was in the audience. He came up to me afterwards, shook my hand and said, "You got it, but a minor point, I don't agree with your definition of entrepreneurship, otherwise, spot on!" Allan has an international academic reputation, and kindly nominated me for my Professorship at Curtin Business School in Perth. His words closed the loop for me on my twenty years of work. Eureka!

I now had academic and entrepreneurial confirmation that my journey to crack the code had paid off.

Here is the **entrecode**® model we developed:

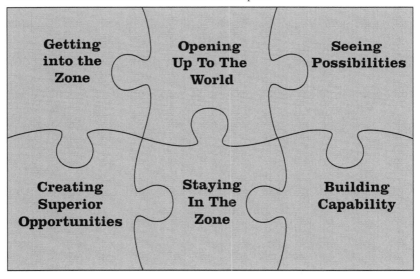

entrecode®

Getting Into The Zone	
The entrepreneurial mindset that creates success	
Factor	Description
Achievement Drive	Acts with determination and purpose to achieve results.
Compelling Vision	A picture of what the end game will look like which is highly motivating.
Goal Directed Energy	High levels of energy to make things happen.
Action Oriented	Takes the initiative and takes actions quickly.

Opening Up To The World
Connecting with the world

Factor	Description
Expressing Passion	Expresses ideas in a highly persuasive and inspiring manner.
Purposeful Networking	Builds and maintains networks of useful business relationships.
Creates Partnerships	Negotiating deals and builds strong commercial partnerships.

Seeing Possibilities
Joining the dots

Factor	Description
Big Picture	Focuses on the strategic big picture.
Options Thinking	Creates a wide range of alternatives to resolve issues.
Savvy	Relies on intuition and experience to guide judgments.

Creating Superior Opportunities
Opportunities which are highly profitable with a sustainable competitive advantage

Factor	Description
Problem Seeking	Seeks to find where customers have a problem the need resolving.
Synthesis	Integrates new information in order to develop new approaches.
Problem Solving	Creates solutions to customers' problems that create new business opportunities.
Delighting Customers	Ensures that the customer's experiences are exceptional.

Staying In The Zone Use it or lose it	
Factor	Description
Focus	Stays focused on priorities, avoiding distractions.
Positive Mindset	Stays positive through all circumstances.
Self-Determining	Comfortable making own decisions which will shape own destiny.
Persistence	Persistent at seeing things through and recovering well from setbacks.

Building Capability Building the business capacity to grow	
Factor	Description
Building the Team	Building a strong team by selecting and motivating the right people.
Ensuring systems and processes are installed	Creating the culture, systems and processes that serve the business.
Experiential Learning	Learns by doing and from successful peers.

The full **entrecode**® is set out in detail in chapter 15.

The journey of discovery was over but the next challenge was to discover whether I could actually use the **entrecode**® to help boost entrepreneurial performance. This would be the validation of whether the code was truly cracked. When reading the entrepreneur's stories that follow, see if you can identify the key entrepreneurial behaviours set out above. This is good practice in building your understanding of the entrepreneurial process and may help you in developing your business.

Lessons Learned

- A key to successful entrepreneurship is getting and staying in the zone. The sports world has understood for many years that high performance in any endeavor is down to mindset.

- High performance skills can be coached and developed, so entrepreneurship is no longer a black art!

- Most successful high growth entrepreneurs serve an apprenticeship where they build networks of contacts and learn how to do business at someone else's expense.

- Being a successful entrepreneur is as much about knowing 'who' as 'how'.

- The **entrecode**® factors are those which are consistently found in high performing people.

- The full **entrecode**® lessons are set out in detail in Chapter 15.

A Rough Road in America

When I signed the deal with Peter Saville I was over the moon. Now we had not only a development process that would build on the new insights but a simple test to indicate the potential for awakening any entrepreneurial skills an individual might possess, the skills we had now identified as critical to success.

But there were still questions that needed answering if my ambition to provide a template that could work anywhere in the world, regardless of language and culture, could become a reality. So I used my business contacts to locate entrepreneurs working in very different business circumstances to those found in Yorkshire or anywhere in the UK. Would the model for understanding entrepreneurs safely pass the tougher tests that might be found elsewhere in the world?

My first lead took me to meet Mike Firth who, although a Yorkshireman, had made his mark on the wider world and set up a company in the USA, apparently with some success. That was before disaster struck.

I travelled to Leeds to meet him in his office, aware of the troubles he had encountered in the States and not quite sure he would have wanted me to open up old battle scars. But I needn't have worried. He greeted me with warmth and enthusiasm and broke the ice by telling me a joke, one that he laughed at as much as I did. In the course of the hour I spent with him he had me in stitches a dozen times or more. It's not the sort of behaviour you would expect from a 65-year-old. His closely shaven head and ruddy cheeks reinforced the impression that deep inside there was still a man in his twenties or thirties striving to get out. Of bitterness and

ill feeling over the American affair I could detect not a trace. Yet for all the joking, Mike gives the impression he has a mind working at 100 miles an hour, picking up ideas and joining the dots to create new business insights. In that sense he was a classic entrepreneur. He came over as a man of vision with boundless energy, a person who could inspire others. He possessed that essential ingredient, drive.

Seventeen years ago he founded the Yorkshire International Business Convention, an annual event that has put Yorkshire on the global map. Keynote speakers have included Bill Clinton, Bob Geldof and Dave Stewart – the last sharing a platform with Mike himself in a duet rendering of *Hoochie Coochie Man*. His female guests have included Elle Macpherson, better known for her modelling talents, but now also known for her knowledge of the world of business and finance.

Nowadays Mike has three or four fledgling businesses on the go and his mind seems to dart between them. I asked him where the ideas came from. "What I do is notice the trends out there. I then create a picture in my mind. Before I know it I have developed the idea into a business opportunity." After ten minutes of our conversation he looks bored, his mind wandering elsewhere. As we have seen, entrepreneurs seem to share this trait. It can be very disconcerting when you first encounter it. But I've found it is nothing personal. If you want to tap into the genius of the best entrepreneurs you have to grin and bear it.

Another quality shown by successful entrepreneurs is an early interest in setting up shop. Mike was born and bred in the market town of Dewsbury, Yorkshire. Like many entrepreneurs he started his business ventures while he was still at school. He would buy firewood for three old pennies a bundle and take them to his customers on a bike with a large basket on the front, making a tidy profit. To top up his earnings he picked and packed rhubarb on Sundays during the growing season. "I suppose I was like my dad, earning money as soon as I got out of the pram."

His father had worked as a small-time entrepreneur from an early age in the Dewsbury 'rag trade'. This had provided an income but involved long hours and hard work. He told me: "He was a successful man, very hard-working. But he didn't get a very good grounding at school. He had to

leave aged 13 when his father died and became the breadwinner. When he was in the company of graduates and such like he felt embarrassed by his lack of education".

It was the lifelong social awkwardness of his father that inspired Mike to get a degree in physics from Bradford University. As we've seen, many entrepreneurs have a tendency to drop out of college. So was getting a degree a good thing or a bad thing for Mike? It certainly led him to follow an initial career path that served as the best possible introduction to man management.

On graduating he went to work for Mars in Slough and was assigned to working on the production line. He was told that he would be promoted to manager when they felt he was ready. The move came sooner than he anticipated – just nine weeks into the job. Suddenly he found himself in charge of 30 people packaging two million Mars Bars per day. He spent four years in all at Mars and although he really enjoyed the experience it did reinforce his early desire to run his own business. The knowledge he gained of the food business opened the way to better things. "Working for Mars proved to be a very useful apprenticeship for my first adventure into business on my own. I always knew, deep down, that I would one day run my own show. In those days I was young, naive and arrogant enough to think I could make a success of it".

After four years at Mars combined with courtship and marriage, he was offered a further promotion. It proved to be a climactic moment of his life. If he accepted the offer he would be drawn inexorably into a management role within a large corporation. If he didn't make the break now he'd be trapped for good. He broke the news to his bewildered wife: "I want to move back to Yorkshire and start a new life. It means resigning from Mars."

"But what will we do?" she asked. Mike gave a typical entrepreneur's reply:

"I'll think of something."

When he told his work colleagues of his decision they thought he had gone mad. But he had a vision of just why he had to leave: "Had I stayed at Mars I would have used the money – which was more than the prime minister

earned – to buy a big house on a big mortgage and that would be it. I'd be a wage slave forever. It was not for me." Mike's faith that something would turn up proved accurate enough. He knew about providing labour and skills for contract packing and so on his return to Leeds he targeted local companies who might be crying out for a new supplier.

It is a classic path that many successful entrepreneurs have chosen to follow. He started with the minimum of resources – no office and still to be connected to the telephone. (This after all was in the late 1960s.) He drove across much of Yorkshire, introducing himself to buyers and talking over the need for a better source of supply. Most turned him down but one at Waddingtons in Leeds gave him an order to pack plastic cups into retail packs. "Where's you're base and I'll send a van to deliver the plastic cups," said the buyer.

This was on Friday and Mike had no warehouse, not even an office. He thought quickly on his feet: "I will call you Monday with the address."

He then spent the weekend desperately organising packing machines and premises and eventually found both. He installed himself in part of a big shed at the old Avro building at Leeds Bradford Airport and recruited a small workforce. Thirty years on, Mike still thinks fondly of that first customer: "The guy at Waddingtons must have seen something in me because I had no money or premises but I was dead keen. Like most entrepreneurs, I got the business first and then worried about how I was going to deliver it later."

A few years down the track Mike got a contract to pack sugar for Billingtons of Liverpool, so he sold his original Co-Packing business and moved seamlessly into the food packaging business. He founded a new company called Normanton Foods and then acquired a mall operation called Hunni Foods, supplying dried fruit for supermarkets. He loved seeing the business grow and grow. By 1990 it had an annual turnover of £15million.

The next step in this example of the entrepreneur at work was to buy up a competitor company for £12 million, funded by a loan from a venture capital company (luckily in this case a good choice). Now he was really

motoring. His new financial director introduced methods to tightly control working which greatly improved his profits. The result was to develop a healthy business with a turnover of £60million. Then the 'city' came calling!

The progress had been startling. But the guardian angel that had brought Mike fortune and contentment, at this point went to sleep on the job. It began well enough. A City financier called Pat O'Reilly crossed his path. O' Reilly, known to some finance journalists as 'Mr Yorkshire' because he specialised in raising capital for Yorkshire companies, persuaded Mike to float the business on the London Stock Exchange to allow him to grow his business.

As we'll see, bringing capital in from outside the business often produces a crisis for many small and not so small companies. Mike Firth found himself involved with City bankers and he was now obliged to go up to London to report progress and answer questions. At the very least it was a distraction that could lead to a damaging loss of focus. Mike hated it: *"Who are these guys?"* he thought.

Mike's new merchant bankers took him to California to buy part of the Del Monte franchise, i.e. the dried fruit business with a turnover of some £100 million. The year was 1993. Before the fall came a moment of hubris. Mike relates the story with a sense of pride: "My business in the UK was now called Yorkshire Foods and in the USA Yorkshire Foods INC. I loved that, taking our culture to the Americans."

But the problem Mike now faced was finding executives who knew how to handle the rough-house tactics brought to bear by his American rivals. To them, he was an unwanted intruder into their territory. A few months after setting up Yorkshire Foods INC, Mike was invited to lunch at a restaurant in Bakersfield, Ca. by the managing director of a rival fruit importing business. Since the company was one of his biggest competitors in the States, Mike felt he was being invited into the lion's den, but he accepted the invitation nevertheless. Maybe this is normal, he thought.

The restaurant turned out to be plush but with only one table set for two people in the centre. "It reminded me like something out of a mafia film,"

said Mike. "The only thing missing was the horse's head." Looking round at the empty tables, Mike enquired: "Quiet today. Is business bad?" It was possibly not the right thing to say.

As if to prove him wrong, his host summoned his personal butler – flown over especially from New York – to serve the aperitifs. Even then Mike did not smell a rat. After an outwardly pleasant lunch, the competitor suddenly looked him straight in the eye and said coldly: "Mike, I need you to stop competing with me or I will finish you."

"You will put me out of business?" enquired a puzzled Mike.

"No, said his competitor, I will finish you – personally!"

Mike was taken aback, laughed out loud, and made his excuses and left.

Before his competitor turned up for that lunch Mike's business had been flourishing and he had floated it as a public company on the stock market in the UK. The future appeared rosy and he relaxed a little, enjoying that feeling of a success well earned: "I was riding high thinking I was a big hitter in the City being courted by investment bankers and city slickers. Wow! I had arrived."

Nothing came of this for a year. Mike had almost forgotten the threat. Then the fates combined to bring him down. Mike began experiencing a 'cash flow' problem, due to the unusually long lag between the sending out an invoice to a customer and the arrival of the cheque to settle the account. This is a very common headache for new businesses, especially if abroad and without a good grasp of the local business culture.

Mike was certainly caught on the back foot. He had to go to his banker in America and seek an overdraft to cover him until the supplier paid up. But this was never to happen. Despite Mike's confidence about the American business the finances were not as sound as he thought. At this juncture his lunching companion chose to reappear on the scene.

Somehow the American had picked up rumours that Mike's business was sailing into stormy waters. Mike was in the throes of renegotiating the terms with his bank when the bank's attitude suddenly hardened. Mike firmly believes his competitor had made a private approach to the

bank to suggest a deal. If the bank called in Mike's assets, so effectively shutting down the business, he promised to step in with an offer to buy the Del Monte assets.

It was a murky affair, compounded by the competitor's slippery nature. When the bank forced Mike into liquidation, the promised counter bid by the competitor failed to materialise, leaving the bank to save what it could from the wreckage. Mike was left without allies, high and dry. He has kept out of the dried fruit trade ever since.

It's an unusual story but it illustrates the difficulties entrepreneurs can encounter on the way to fortune – the road does not always run smoothly, especially when the business is operating in a foreign land where the business textbook on business ethics may be serving as a door stop in a forgotten back corridor. Mike showed his mettle by launching his new enterprises in his native Yorkshire. To his credit, Mike never saw any of these experiences as failures. 'Entrepreneurs don't fail, businesses fail' remains his time-hardened view of the world. What Mike meant was entrepreneurs usually give it their best shot but something happens outside of their control which harms the business and it may even fail. So the business has failed but not the entrepreneur and I agree with his assessment.

No one ever said running your own business is always fun. There are many pitfalls on the road to success. That's why persistence is the cardinal virtue in the entrepreneur's bible. But persistence needs a source of energy to keep it alive. During my years of working with entrepreneurs I've seen time and time again just how important an inner drive can be if the obstacles in the way of dream fulfilment are to be successfully overcome. This is a truism that applies, in my experience, to every sort of start-up business in Britain.

Lessons Learned

- Try to serve an apprenticeship at someone else's expense to reduce the risks when starting your business.

- The ability to recover from setbacks, you can see once again, is a key entrepreneurial skill.

- A compelling vision keeps entrepreneurs going and provides focus and direction for all their activities.

- Keep your eyes on the competition at all times.

- Try to maintain a positive mental attitude, particularly when the going gets tough.

- Make sure you keep the bank and investors on side – you and they don't want any surprises.

- Successful entrepreneurs are highly driven, possess masses of energy and are extremely action orientated.

- **The entrecode® principles are universal across countries and cultures.**

Chapter Nine
The Sydney Harbour Bridge Climb

Like almost all the successful entrepreneurs I know, Paul Cave was driven by passion. He was primarily motivated to find a way to offer everyone who came to Sydney, or already lived there, a chance to take up the challenge of climbing up the steel superstructure of the Sydney Harbour Bridge, one of the wonders of the modern world and hitherto a no-go area to all but the maintenance staff. Perhaps, he thought, there might even be a viable business in doing that.

At first glance it was a bizarre idea. The girders of the bridge were never intended to be climbed in this way by a constant stream of climbing parties who would need supervision and support. It was built in the inter-war years to improve links between north and south Sydney, a giant steel archway across the harbour that straddles the deep waters below. It remains today the widest and heaviest, and one of the longest, single arch bridge of its type, carrying eight lanes of traffic and a double track railway line. The idea of giving adventurous members of the public access to the dizzying heights of the bridge steel work - high enough at 134 metres above water to reduce those using the bridge below to resemble little more than ants - had never occurred to anyone until Paul confided in some business associates that he had a plan to transform the bridge in the public imagination, adding a fourth major Australian tourist attraction to the already well-established trio of 'the Rock, the Reef and the Sydney Opera House'.

When Paul came up with this idea for the 'BridgeClimb' in 1989 he had already anticipated that there would be resistance and opposition from those who saw the bridge as an icon and wanted to protect it and keep it

the way it was. But Paul had an obsessive side to his character and was ready to rise to the challenge. As we will see, it was his entrepreneurial passion and his ability to bounce back from numerous setbacks that brought him ultimate victory.

His obsession with the bridge dated back to a gift he received on his 40th birthday from his father-in-law, who passed away shortly afterwards. It was a train ticket numbered 0001, the very first ticket issued to a railway passenger when the bridge opened on 20th March 1932. To lay hands on this ticket his father-in law - then a teenager - had camped out for two days with his brother and a shared blanket to make sure they were first in the queue when the doors of Wynyard Railway Station opened at 5 am.

"If it hadn't been for that ticket," Paul relates, "the Harbour Bridge Climb would never have happened. When my father-in-law died, something of that bridge obsession passed to me."

Paul had already proved himself adept as an entrepreneur, having founded Amber Tiles, a tile and paving business that offered free training in the rudiments of laying tiles. Thanks to this formula, and the excellent customer service that went with it, the firm had grown from nothing to become Australia's largest tile company. In Paul's own words, he is first and foremost an entrepreneur, who said he probably stayed on at Amber "a few years beyond my use-by date".

In 1989, Sydney was to play host to a convention of the Young Presidents Organisation, the YPO, an international network of youthful business executives. Paul soon became involved in organising the event, and came up with an idea that would offer the delegates a chance to socialise, make friends and enjoy a memorable shared experience.

While discussing a list of possibilities with Nick Greiner, the former Prime Minister of New South Wales (himself an enthusiastic supporter of the YPO), the notion of giving delegates an opportunity to climb to the top of the Harbour Bridge was raised. Paul volunteered to find out whether it was even worth considering - after all, there would be more than 600 delegates who would need to be marshalled into groups and supervised as they headed for the top, using the existing network of exposed metal

stairs, gantries and ladders that would test even the strongest nerves.

Armed with contact details, he headed for the southern abutment tower of the bridge, which housed the bridge maintenance offices, to meet the foreman, carrying with him a selection of his bridge mementos. He had reckoned these might help break the ice during the meeting.

He found the foreman in his office and spent half an hour showing and discussing his items, and exchanging bridge stories. Only then did he reveal what he had in mind. Paul explained it was to give these bosses of the future the chance to have a bonding experience they would never forget. The foreman was not exactly wild about the idea, and not entirely persuaded that it would be possible to take 600 youngish business people on such an expedition.

"You know, the bosses are often the ones who are the greatest wimps," he told Paul.

Paul politely begged to differ. "I'm not so sure you are right about that," he said. The foreman stood his ground: "People often freak out up there, and we have to take them off, disrupting our workers." Perhaps to test Paul's conviction, or perhaps his resolve, he curled up his finger and said abruptly: "You come with me."

Twenty years on, Paul still has vivid memories of that summons. "I will never forget that crooked finger. The foreman was wearing a grey boiler suit and work boots. I was wearing leather shoes and a suit. I thought he might give me some overalls. But we just started to walk."

Paul felt the foreman was daring him to follow him up onto the bridge. The dare wasn't without precedent, as Paul knew. In a famous court case over the wage rates paid while the bridge was being built, the judge had been invited to climb up to see where the men worked. Unwisely, he took up the challenge and didn't get far in his suit and shoes. He famously pronounced in favour of the workers: "Give them what they asked for."

Would Paul make it to the top? Or confirm his 'wimp' status in the eyes of the foreman?

He relates what happened: "I followed him to the kingpost ladder (the

point where the climb starts) only too aware of the foreman's sturdy boots and my flimsy shoes. Then we began to climb in earnest. I told myself 'This is crazy, don't do this'. So many things were playing out in my head and stomach and my heart. My knees were shaking, and my knuckles white, my shoes were slipping … and I just may have wet my pants a little as I climbed that ladder! When we got to the top, a couple of workers ran across one of the horizontal beams. They are only eight inches wide. My jaw dropped."

A conversation and a relationship with the foreman had begun, and gradually, by listening to concerns and discussing and testing solutions, the foreman went along with the idea. The main concern was to keep the danger to a minimum. The delegates would go up with an RTA guide, and in groups of no more than four at a time. By the time the convention descended on the city the plans were in place. During the day set aside for the climb, Paul shadowed delegates with their guides - they had been fully briefed before setting out - and watched them climb and descend with growing confidence, positively glowing at their achievement. He gradually realised that it might be possible to share this not only with business executives but with everyone. Paul describes his Eureka moment: "A light bulb went on when I witnessed the response of the delegates to that climb. It inspired me to consider opening up to the public at large."

This became his vision, one that he kept with him over the next nine years as he strove to make the dream a reality.

Paul sold Amber in a management buyout in 1994 when he finally realised he needed to clear the decks and focus 100% of his time on making BridgeClimb happen.

One of his first concerns was that word of the idea might leak out and he would see himself pipped at the post by a rival entrepreneur. He had to act quickly to protect his vision. This involved putting together a confidentiality agreement for all parties he needed to consult in preparing his proposal, and considering whether elements of the idea could be patented or not.

Paul looks back now with some pride on the loyalty of the staff he recruited to the project: "Initially I reckoned we could have the whole business up and running in two years or so. I recruited a team with the range of skills we would need and asked them all to sign a sweeping confidentiality agreement, regardless of rank or experience. In the years it actually took to develop the plan, not a single detail slipped out."

The first big challenge - to avoid being overtaken by rival bids - was thus seen off. Now the serious business of hammering out an agreement between the company and the public bodies responsible for looking after the bridge could begin.

When the initial business plan was complete Paul presented it to all the relevant authorities, which included the NSW Roads and Traffic Authority - commonly known as the RTA and the body responsible for the bridge itself and all the paraphernalia that goes with road traffic management - and the State Rail Authority (SRA), which had responsibility for the tracks and the rail services.

In 1994, Paul and his team had their first formal meeting with the authorities to discuss their proposal. Internal consultations within the public authorities followed, and while the business plan had taken an optimistic line - stressing the great opportunity to create new jobs and open up a new source of income for the NSW government - the reaction from the authorities left Paul in no doubt that there would be significant hurdles to overcome. Their response was to submit a list of 'issues and concerns' that had to be addressed - some sixty-four in all. It was a daunting reply, and made it clear the grand vision that had focused the minds of Paul's team did not initially strike a chord with the authorities who were to make the final decisions.

Paul looks back on it as a time of frustration and stress. He confesses: "I probably would never have started out on this journey had I known what lay ahead."

But he found a way through, firstly by putting himself in the shoes of his opponents: "While we were fired by having a world first on our hands and by pioneering something new, the BridgeClimb concept understandably

presented a significant challenge to conventional thinking."

Paul looked for ways in which he might win over the ranks of sceptics to the cause, and came up with a way of turning the 'issues and concerns' list into a working 'menu'.

"Having this menu to work with we could address the issues one by one. We were able to demonstrate ways in which we could overcome the multitude of problems that had to be tackled. These stretched from safety concerns - where objects might be dropped causing accidents, where train drivers and motorists could be distracted by climbers - to where walkways and handrails would impact on bridge heritage, how painters could get on with their job of painting the bridge and so on."

Using this strategy meant slow progress, but each issue could be properly addressed and a solution found, one by one, until - they hoped - all sixty-four items (and more that were raised along the way) could be satisfactorily resolved and the way opened for the vision finally to become a reality.

Persistence and problem solving, I maintain, are two of the cardinal virtues of the successful entrepreneur. How had Paul managed to cope with the ups and downs he encountered in pursuit of his vision? He told me: "Always look for the silver lining in the setback. Each setback in the BridgeClimb saga became a new opportunity for more research and a challenge to regroup and look at things differently. BridgeClimb would have been a very different business had we been able to commence operating after two years. We had to take the extra time to complete the additional research and carefully consider each and every objection or problem in order to overcome them. In the end this enriched the business."

So it was that some six years were spent winkling out problems, clarifying what they were and finding solutions to them.

Sometimes there was no easy solution. But a man or woman driven by a grand vision will be prepared to go that extra mile to turn frustration into fulfilment and triumph. This was certainly the case with the most intractable problem, one that took more than a year of concentrated

effort and discussion to untangle: the issue of high-visibility jackets.

Over the years, the safety of bridge workers had been a constant concern. To reduce accidents and save lives, all staff working close to the railway tracks had been obliged to wear bright yellow over jackets to maximise their visibility to oncoming trains. Setting out from sea level to climb to the top was bound to bring the climbers into close contact with the railway tracks and the overhead wiring.

So should the climbers be obliged to don orange jackets? At this point, the safety concerns of the Rail Corp clashed with those of the RTA, which was worried that climbers high among the girder work would distract motorists crossing the bridge, and that the bright colours would impact on the traditional grey aesthetic of the bridge. To reduce the dangers they wanted to follow a policy of climbers wearing 'low-visibility' garments. Paul had earlier reassured the authorities that all climbers would have to wear weatherproof one-piece climbing suits in a dull grey and blue to address those concerns. Now the guardians of the road and the guardians of the railway found themselves locked in an impasse.

Looking back on the controversy Paul can smile, but it was a real issue at the time. "Both arms of the bureaucracy were right," he now argues.

"The rules about high-visibility jackets had been set out very clearly and it appears that nobody was willing to use their discretion to look at the original intent of the rule and stick their head above the parapet and say, 'Hey what they are proposing will meet the real concern and we can grant you an exemption'. We learned it was inevitably better not to challenge the rules but to patiently demonstrate how we would comply with the intent behind them, to not be a threat but a provider of solutions. Or even better, to encourage and help lead the authority to be the solution providers, most importantly to make it easy for the authorities to ultimately say 'Yes'."

The solution in the end was that the climbers, although following a route close to the railway, would be tethered and secured to a safety line, and could therefore never get close enough to be in any danger.

So by 1998 all of the 'concerns and issues' had been dealt with, each

solved by an exercise in reason and an atmosphere of mutual respect. The list of amendments to the original plan was agreed and the changes put in place.

Of course, the long process of winning approval for the new tourist attraction made things difficult financially for the lead pioneer. Paul had initially put several million dollars of his own cash into the company, long before the first paying customer could climb the bridge. He had brought four of his business colleagues into an initial circle of investors in 1991. One of them, the music entrepreneur Brett Blundy, put up additional cash and ultimately introduced a new investor, Jack Cowin.

During the process of looking for other investors, Paul had made some forty presentations to both private and established investment institutions. "All thought BridgeClimb was a great idea, but when push came to shove it wasn't a proven business. There were some, who were afraid of heights, who simply couldn't conceive that anyone would pay to do this!" He reports that since the company became profitable and well-established many of those would-be investors are now kicking themselves, and others emerged from the woodwork after the event, offering to invest. But with the steady flow of revenue since BridgeClimb opened for business in 1998 there has been little need for any external investment. The cost of a ticket is now A$198 per person.

Paul has continued in his role as Chairman of BridgeClimb since the business began operating, but allows management to get on with running the business, very much in line with his philosophy that good entrepreneurs do not generally make good long-term managers. However, he takes a keen interest in the firm, and was pleased to see it rise into the top ten of the 'places I want to see before I die' list.

In 2012, the power of the business to gather free publicity was underlined by a flying visit to BridgeClimb by the celebrated American TV star Oprah Winfrey.

Year on year the business has taken off, forcing the company to provide extra climbs, including the very popular dawn and sunset slots. The view is just heavenly say the fans.

Lessons Learned

What were the key lessons Paul Cave learned from the BridgeClimb experience?

- Always be prepared for knockbacks or potential diversions. Go back, do a bit more homework, and come at it again.

- Recipe for Success? Find something different and unique. Keep it simple.

- Focus your offering. Recognise the unique value you deliver. Don't try to be all things. Be famous for just one thing.

- Deliver quality every time. Let nothing fall between the cracks.

- Listen. Really listen. Celebrate when you receive criticism and complaints. You have been gifted an opportunity to improve.

- Sometimes it's best not to know what you may be getting yourself into, or you would otherwise never start!

I asked Paul Cave what Entrecode factors he felt had helped him become successful.

- Compelling Vision

- Expressing Passion

- Creating Partnerships (Win/Win)

- Options Thinking

- Savvy

- Problem Seeking (My job description was to find the one thing that would stop this from happening.)

- Problem Solving (Most often you will not be the one with the answers. The one that experiences the problem is most often the one that does.)

- Persistence

- Building a Team (Recognise your own weaknesses and surround

yourself with people that are better than you at doing things.)

- Take a personal interest in customer feedback; set the culture for those around you and be the one that closes the loop.

- **The entrecode® principles are universal across countries and cultures.**

Chapter Ten
Woman in Command

The spread of Western management methods to what were only recently considered 'third world' countries has been remarkable. Take India for example. Just three years ago Tom Peters the celebrated 'business guru' came on a whirlwind tour of the sub-continent – staging conferences in Delhi and Mumbai. Feedback from star-struck admirers flooded in. This is how a typical participant reacted on the online pages of the Times of India:

Hi, Tom Peters was awesome!! I wish he had gone on for more time!! It was the first time I heard him and has surely left a mark on how I will be leading my company in the future!!

The rapturous reception given to Tom Peters was as good a sign as any that India meant business. As the western world slumped into recession in 2008 India was set to power ahead.

Sitting in the audience as Peters challenged businesses everywhere to embrace his messages that the customer was king and women more economically powerful than ever before was youthful looking Veena Patil. Veena was being groomed to take over her father's business and had come along to soak in the Peters experience. He was the architect of the quest for excellence in business, preaching the fervent slogan: productivity through people. Veena could take comfort from her belief that she was on the right track, as managing director of an offshoot of her father's travel business.

Her father, Kesari Patil, was in his 70s and was looking ahead. Who would take over from him when he retired or passed on? Whilst all the

family really helped and pulled together to support their father, Veena, the oldest of his four children, was chosen to lead what had become one of India's fastest growing travel businesses. The business started in 1984 with a pledge *When we make a promise to our guests we keep it,* "A firm belief in honest and transparent deals, no hidden costs and striving for 100 percent customer satisfaction are the ways we try to ensure we keep our promises," Veena told me.

Kesari Patil, then aged 49, had decided to give up his job as a tourist guide working for his brother's firm and start up on his own. In classic entrepreneur tradition, he had learnt his craft working with his brother and now created an enterprise with little or no capital at his disposal. His wife had made him a gift of her jewellery to help him get started. The business was set up in his home, a cramped chawl in a tenement, just ten feet by ten feet.

Mr Patil hired a coach and gathered 13 'explorers' who wanted to take an adventure trip to Rajasthan, the desert state that's home to camels and forts. On his first trip he set a precedent that was followed for years to come. He personally went on the trip to make it special, to make sure the customers got absolute satisfaction. Tom Peters, I suspect, would have approved.

The company survived its first year, but only just. All the modest profit went to pay off the debts. Only the fact that his wife and daughters serviced the office while he combined the role of director with that tourist guide, kept it going.

But he had caught a rising tide. With the Indian population then nigh on a billion and a growing middle-class, more and more Indians wanted the excitement of exploration. Kesari Travel and Tours grew and grew. That's not to say it was an easy ride. The main demand for those first tours was to visit Kashmir, a beautiful Himalayan province with a heritage of conflict. When fighting broke out in the late 80s the tourists switched their attention elsewhere. With hindsight, it was probably a good thing for the future of the company. The firm could see the advantages in diversifying, arranging for trips across the sub-continent and then venturing out to bring in the globe. By 2012 Kesari Tours was running

conducted tours across all seven continents. The family firm was now worth millions of rupees.

The business was not one you might expect to find in India if you still have the image of a third world country in your mind. Mr Patil's business had taken off with 14 branch offices scattered across the world, including one in London. The company catered for the growing Indian middle-class, determined to enjoy package holidays not only in India but in faraway lands. The holidays were adventurous by any standard. For instance, there was the option of flying to Switzerland for a whirlwind dash through the Alps, on cable cars and alpine railways mixed with shopping in Geneva, and Zurich. Even more remarkable was the tour that took Indians to the 'land of the midnight sun' travelling through Norway and Finland to experience summer north of the Arctic Circle, and south to the Antarctic, avoiding the baking heat and tropical downpours of India.

Successful as it was the big question remained. Kesari was now in his 70s and wanted to pass the business on to the family. But who was to take charge and provide the leadership? At one level the choice seemed easy; Veena was the eldest of the children and had shown she had a good business brain. She had already helped her father run the company. She had also made a name for herself as a travel writer (like her father she had acted as guide and mentor on many tours). On the other hand, she had been raised in a little village some 110 kilometres from Mumbai, a village with no running water and no electricity. The village school had one teacher who divided her attention among children of all ages. Perhaps not surprisingly, Veena felt herself lacking in confidence, rather shy and withdrawn.

Mumbai was a city pulsing with energy. It was a perfect place to make contacts and exchange business ideas. If Veena was to shake off her lack of confidence, there was no better place to do it. Of course, Kesari was to bring the rest of the family to live close to the city while he presided over the growth of the company. The family worked together relentlessly to support their father. When Kesari thought he might start to take it easy, it was his eldest daughter who urged him to push on and build new markets. Following the success of the international business, other

companies sprang up to offer much the same. What was needed was a new vision of how to build a future for the company that would take account of the rapid social changes that had gripped India. In brief, there was a fragmentation of the one big market into dozens of smaller specialised markets – such as holidays for newlyweds, students, the active elderly – and the not so active; as well as people intent on going on pilgrimage, and even 'for men only'.

Veena had become rather good at advocacy – surprising those who knew her by making a speech at her graduation in which she made a bold statement that life had to be lived beyond the mundane. Now, as she matured, she could argue for her ideas and take responsibility in developing them.

The push towards the niche markets brought a spurt in growth. Kesari took the opportunity to give her a chance to show her entrepreneurial skills. Could this self-confessed 'introvert' make a go of running a part of the company? Was there an untapped market waiting to be served? Veena thought there was.

Veena told me, "My role seven years back was to give the definite roles to each family member to avoid recurring friction as everybody was looking into everything. I tried hard to get the best out of each family member according to their expertise and strength; one was given IT, one was given spiritual tours, another one was given tailor-made holidays... and so on. It was not an easy task, with a lot of stress at the initial stages, but I could do it and everyone accepted it when they understood and saw the success of it."

"Another key part of my role was to bring corporate governance to all functions and procedures and to focus directors, managers, secondary line and junior Kesarians. Also to cascade the vision and mission among all the Kesarians by 'walking the talk'. Kesarians would not have believed or followed me if I had not shown integrity towards Kesari."

In other words, Veena provided strategic leadership to the family business.

In conversation with some of the younger and professional women of Mumbai there was much complaint about the restraints on travel

for young women – and not so young women -- faced. Why couldn't someone challenge the widespread convention that women could not go on holiday on their own or even with women friends? Why not have charter flights and cruises for **women only**. In the west, such a plan would raise few eyebrows. But India is a giant country with a huge range of values. It stands with one foot in ancient tradition and the other in the dynamic fast-changing world of high technology and the Internet.

These cultures overlap in a curious way, particularly for women. Traditionally women have been expected not to go travelling without their husbands. Women travelling alone might be subject to harassment or worse. Young women in particular were seen to be at physical and moral risk. It is a taboo, Veena thought, which ought to be broken. Through her contacts in Mumbai she reckoned there were many, many, younger and professional women who would relish the opportunity to enjoy a holiday with other women. She put the idea down on paper, explaining in detail how the women could rest assured their enjoyment would not be spoiled. Hotels would be carefully chosen and they'd be chaperoned at all times by tour staff whenever they wanted to explore away from the hotel.

The paper and Veena's defence of it convinced old Mr Patil that the idea was feasible and financially sound. He passed the job of masterminding the operation to Veena. Just do it. All the same it was seen as a very risqué idea and Veena didn't rush out immediately to sell it to the world. First she conducted a customer attitude survey and found to their surprise that many husbands would be happy to see their wives go off on such a jaunt. The staff entrusted with the delicate task of making a success of this new all-women trip (and including Veena herself) were given training and encouraged to come up with their own ideas on just what social activities should be laid on. It would have been disastrous if the women guests had come home complaining that the trip had been a bore. The danger of this happening was warded off by a packed schedule.

Veena rose to the challenge. She personally was to lead the first tour, a tour of Thailand. Under the name of the *My Fair Lady* tour, and under the command of Veena, newly appointed MD of My Fair Lady Tours,

over 350 women went on the first of these new concept 'niche' trips. The experience produced a marked change in Veena's body language as she relaxed and got to know the travellers. On arrival that first evening she stood up and addressed the large audience, giving a warm welcome to the guests. She sat down to applause and surely felt a distinct and satisfying sense of personal ownership. Thereafter she posted a daily newsletter giving them a cheerful and charming thought for the day. Veena's overall verdict summed up what this revolutionary tour of Thailand had done for the guests:

"Most ladies have reported that their lives have been transformed ever since they travelled on this tour. For the first time in their lives they are completely free of their day-to-day responsibilities and...this gives them the feeling that they too are cared for and have a life of their own. Life on this tour is nothing less than a celebration of womanhood".

Since the launch of the *My Fair Lady* tours, the company has moved into a period of faster growth, seeing off the mounting competition from western cut-price airlines and others. Veena put it down to having a good offer and making 'customer delight' the very top priority – a mantra inculcated in every member of staff. Kesari Tours is the first travel company in the world to be certified for Quality and Health and Safety standards of ISO. This certification is tough to acquire and maintain for such a large service organisation.

But just as important has been the strategic thinking Veena has invested in the running of the expanded company. She soon moved up to become Managing Director of Kesari Tours, an empire that grew steadily as the company introduced 'Specialty Tours', a whole series of niche products that have secured, for the moment at least, the future of the company.

Veena, now aged 47, has become a symbol of how India's women can make a massive contribution to maintaining the country's steady progress towards becoming a commercial giant. But by anyone's standards it's been a testing time. The last few years have had more than their share of natural disasters. Some of the major problems she has faced include floods, earthquake, volcanic ash, and other such calamities.

Veena is a natural entrepreneur. She demonstrates a clear vision, and has a driving passion and energy. It hardly needs saying that she has the entrepreneur's knack of possessing a unique entrepreneurial ability to recover from setbacks. Her unique approach to developing her business has been classically entrepreneurial, as we have discovered on our journey thus far to crack the code.

"We go out of our way to find customer problems and then solve them." Veena told me. "These solutions become our new tour offerings. Feedback from the guests plays a major role in maintaining that strategy. We are not the cheapest but we offer quality year after year. If you give people what they really want they are willing to pay that bit more." Veena has grown her business to employ 750 people in 14 offices and another 450 tour managers around the world. She told me: "We have grown by developing our people and encouraging them to be creative. That way we can stay ahead of the opposition and develop the innovations that will keep us keep ahead."

"I encourage them to take their own decisions and to take responsibility for them. When they hit a problem we do not blame anybody. Our view is to find out why it happened and then make sure it does not happen again. I have had to let go and trust people in order to grow our company."

No one can predict the future with any accuracy, but her positive mindset, her drive and energy, and her leadership qualities are assets that Kesari Tours are very lucky to have. Her presence at the heart of the action, her unflappability at all times is the single greatest asset the company has. She is resilience personified. With her contribution to making the world becoming a better place, she is behaving as all the very best entrepreneurs strive to behave. That's why I really enjoyed talking with Veena, her passion and energy is infectious. She is one of those entrepreneurs who remind me why I love what I do for a living. I am convinced we shall hear more of her.

Having proven that the **entrecode**® principles have international relevance in helping businesses to grow and prosper, my next challenge was to see if the principles we followed in starting and growing a business

can be of any use in rejuvenating tired old companies that are presently on the road to nowhere.

Lessons Learned

- Create new profitable opportunities by developing products for market segments not currently served.

- A compelling vision keeps entrepreneurs going and provides focus and direction for all their activities.

- Successful entrepreneurs are highly driven, possess masses of energy and are extremely action orientated.

- Provide the leadership to build the capability of the business in order to grow successfully.

- The **entrecode**® principles are universal across countries and cultures.

Chapter Eleven
The Magic of the Code. Bringing New Life to Old Businesses

Paul Mackie revitalised his business and in doing so created new value. He used every tool in the **entrecode**® *toolbox. Be under no illusion, this is an entrepreneurial story, not a management case study.*

In the spring of 2012 a visitor to Bradford, West Yorkshire, could have been forgiven for thinking a bomb had hit the place. A large chunk of the town centre had disappeared, swallowed up by what the locals referred to as 'the big hole'. It's a terrible warning to those who put their faith in councils and developers: the best laid plans can go horribly wrong.

The promoters of the scheme, the Australian retail giant, Westfield, had put forward a grandiose vision of a giant shopping centre and leisure complex and got the backing of the council in 2006. Then the bulldozers rolled in and flattened the site, only for the developers to call a halt in 2009 because of the credit crunch and the recession that followed. Now at last Westfield and Marks and Spencer are planning a less ambitious scheme. It's some consolation but not enough to secure the future, Paul Mackie told me when I visited him in his Bradford office. "We're entering into probably the toughest five years of business we have ever seen, certainly in the last 150 years since the industrial revolution," he said in an article in the Yorkshire Post newspaper.

"This new world that's emerging, we don't know what's coming out yet. When I think of these global challenges we've got, in America, Europe, the Middle East and the Far East, only the strong will survive," he continued.

Paul is Chairman at the firm of Rex Procter & Partners (or RPP as it is now called). The business provides surveying, project management

and other services to the construction industry. As with many mature companies, it has had to adjust to a fast changing world and had not found it easy. His success at building a team spirit, rooting out outdated practices, and restoring pride to the company has marked him out as a man of the future in Bradford. He's now vice-president of the local Chamber of Commerce and spearheading a drive to revitalise the Bradford economy.

The original surveying firm was founded by Rex Procter, a man who was to make his mark on Bradford and Leeds, but more in sporting circles than in the field of business. Rex was a bit of character. In his twenties he had travelled to work in the Sudan to work alongside canal engineers and dam-builders on a massive project to divert the waters of the Blue Nile to conserve Egypt's water supply. When he returned home, still under the age of 30, he set up the company that bore his name. Known simply as Rex Procter and Partners, it opened its first office at 24 Queen Street, Leeds, in 1937.

The small staff, including three partners and two apprentices, was housed in a Victorian building with oak-panelled rooms, the walls lined with ledgers and professional reference books. It was not to change much in the next 40 years. A second office opened in Bradford in 1973 in a 60s office block.

Rex was a publicly recognised figure, a councillor, a freeman of Kingston upon Hull, and of course a rugby league fan. He had risen to become chairman of the Leeds Rugby League Club. A few weeks before Leeds won the National League Final in 1961 – after a wait of 66 years – he was killed in a car crash. The fans observed a minute's silence before the match began.

Without his leadership the company endured years of stagnation. The office at 24 Queen Street in Leeds was already showing its age. Inside the bookshelves gave the office a distinct musty smell. The strip lighting was harsh and soul-less, the offices, inside and out, were badly in need of a lick of paint. The partners – there were now six of them – acted almost as independent entities. They were fond of entertaining clients on the golf-course. Others gave the impression they were doing prospective clients a

favour by agreeing to discuss business at all.

Paul joined a Bradford surveying business but left three weeks before Christmas. At the time he had one small boy and his wife Paula was pregnant. "Darling," he said, "I have some good news and some bad news. The good news is that I have been offered a partnership, the bad news is I have resigned!" That is when he moved to RPP and quickly worked his way up.

In 1997 he became an equity partner and in 2004 joint senior partner. When he took over as chairman in 2008 he realised he would have a struggle on his hands to drag the business into the 21st century.

He had come across my book on entrepreneurship, *In the Company of Heroes*, and thought I might be able to help win the battle. He called me up and we agreed to meet quietly at his head office. The office had a sad Dickensian air about it. He told me, "You expected at any moment some old chap carrying a surveyor's stick to tramp through, with the mud from the building site still sticking to his boots. We were professional but very old- fashioned. When I took the job as chairman, I thought it's now or never."

I was delighted to take on a consulting role. It gave me a chance to show the **entrecode**® techniques could be applied not just to small or medium-sized, start-up businesses but to mature (even elderly) companies wanting to recapture their youth. Having Paul at the head of the enterprise was a good start. He had a commanding presence, and the air of being a leader. Paul gets up at 4:45am each day and is in the office by 5:30am and works until 6:00pm – successful entrepreneurs work hard. But now we had to decide just where to begin.

It is never easy to turn a company around after it has sat comfortably on its hands for years. It involved changing the way the whole staff thought and acted. There could be pitfalls ahead. I had some inkling of what could yet trip Paul up when he confided in me: "The most annoying thing is to make a suggestion on how we might change our long-established working practices and culture and replace them with something more modern only to be told: "We don't do things that way here.""

But with Paul leading the operation we maximised our chances of success. There was something about his character that made him rise to a challenge. He had already proved himself by battling against the odds to become a surveyor. As so often in the case with entrepreneurs, he had not done well at school. He had struggled with reading and writing.

He told me the story: "I know now I was dyslexic. But there was no allowance made for it. I left without an O level to my name and failed my A levels. I was great at sport at school and captained the rugby, basketball and football teams. I even captained the teacher's team. This is where I learnt something about leadership, building a team and driving success. The only prize I got was the Dick Pollard Prize for Sports Achievement!"

Paul's first experience of being entrepreneurial was when he was 13. "We had no money; Mum was on her own so I decided to do something about it. My friend and I started a business; Max and Sam Gardening Services. We produced a business card which we cheekily reproduced with the Debenhams logo. People thought we were a legitimate business and we made money".

He was lucky to be taken on as a quantity surveyor. He was doubly lucky that he took a job in Saudi Arabia. "I had real difficultly with writing and spelling because I thought I was dyslexic. My dad left us when I was five. I met him again when I was 26 and he noticed I was writing with my right hand. He said, "I see you are still writing with your right hand, you were left-handed as a young boy but I forced you to write with your right hand." I could have killed him! I immediately started to practise writing with my left hand. Paula, my wife, used to produce pages of letters in dot form and I practised every night joining them up. After three or four months I could write pretty well."

Paul came back to Bradford, his confidence greatly improved. He started his own business on his return but quickly took up a role as a surveyor with a Bradford surveying firm. "My wage did not cover my mortgage then but I was due a bonus of £10K. One day my managing partner told me I had been elected a partner – congratulations – and it would cost me £10K. I left and was lucky to secure a post against stiff competition with

Rex Procter. He married his childhood sweetheart Paula, whom he has known since he was twelve. Then began the short wait to rise to the top.

I began my work with Paul by concentrating on a key factor – the way in which regular and prospective customers were treated by the company. "Do you treat your customers well?" I asked.

"Well, I think so," he replied. "We don't get many complaints."

It is the easiest error to make, to assume a lack of complaints means customer satisfaction. People simply vote with their feet. And Rex Procter was certainly suffering a decline in customer numbers. When I expressed this view he immediately jumped in: "So what should we do to find out what our customers really think?" It sounds embarrassingly easy. "You start with a customer perception survey."

When I mention the customer survey as a tool that might start the ball rolling, there are always some people who look hesitant. But as I explained to him there's really nothing to fear. Most customers are often only too pleased to let off some steam or heap praise on the staff. For a start, the best way to proceed is to send a letter out to your major customers, telling them what you propose to do. A proven way to get honest customer feedback is by telephone. They will tell you things on the phone they would never put in writing or tell you face to face. The telephone method is like a truth drug! We asked the key customers what they looked for in a supplier and how they rated RPP and their competitors out of 10 on the buying criteria they had told us. We also asked what RPP could do to help them solve their current problems. When I called back two weeks later Paul and I considered the average outcome scores. Here are the results of the survey, all ratings out of ten:

	Our Rating	Competitor's Rating
Relationships	8.6	6.2
Technical Skills	8.1	4.5
Professionalism	9.0	3.6
Competence	8.5	5.0

Reasons to be cheerful, Paul thought. Who would have believed that the older firm would have outscored its much larger rivals? RPP had a clear competitive advantage that could be exploited to their own advantage. But what we had measured was only one side of the picture, I suggested. The next step was to conduct a second survey, this time on staff attitudes towards the business. For this to be of great value you need all the staff to be involved, all 120 of them. And to get the best results the survey should be conducted without names being added to the form. (Who wants to bad-mouth their boss openly?)

When the staff survey had been completed, the results were as follows:

Do you feel valued and equipped to do your job?	Average score	80%
Do you know what is expected of you in your job?	Average score	60%
How would you rate your manager?	Average score	53%
Do you have a real pride in working for the business?	Average score	81%

For a full explanation of the assessment system, see *The Hallmarks for Successful Business* pages 32–35.)

The conclusion? This was by no means a lost cause, but the firm could and had to do much better if it were to survive in the long-term. It required the right leadership and much greater staff involvement. The surveys had helped identify blind spots – often a real eye-opener. They also indicated that the company as a whole lacked a proper strategy, a weakness that had to be addressed and addressed quickly.

While young and small companies can usually make decisions quickly, older and larger businesses often get entangled in a combination of red tape and too many layers of management. So a company like RPP had to learn how to respond quickly, delegating decisions to the staff wherever it could. It helped to have strong and charismatic leadership at the top,

as Paul was to prove again and again. His first action was to call together his two most trusted managers (with me as adviser) to decide just what strategy we ought to follow.

I felt an air of excitement as I tackled the first priority – the creation of a statement of mission, vision and values for the company. Such a statement defines the core business the company is in, what it aspires to do – an aspiration powered by an attainable vision of what our role will be in the future and a statement of the company values that will guide all who work for it.

My experience has been that many companies adopt the statement of mission, vision, and values as a token of modernity without much being done to promote it within the company. If that's the case in any business, you can be sure the staff will very soon become cynical and sideline it, effectively banishing it to the trash can. But if the top management warmly embrace it and transmit the message throughout the business, it can become a super-charger that immediately begins to pay dividends, not only in terms of cash, but in terms of staff commitment and customer satisfaction. "The new strategy drives our business. If people ask "should we do this", I say "refer to our mission, vision and values – the clues are there," says Paul.

Of course that depends on crafting a crisp and inspiring set of principles that will govern the business' behaviour at all levels and become its DNA.

This is what Paul and His Team came up with:

Our Mission (*What business are we in?*)
Delivering professional solutions to the property industry

Our Vision (*What do we want to achieve?*)
- Be the business of choice for professionals
- Exceed our client's expectations
- Provide our clients with 'value for money' solutions
- Deliver cost effective and environmentally friendly solutions
- Provide national coverage
- Be the leading construction consultancy in our field

Our Values *(How do we want to do business?)*

- Quality and first-class service at all stages of the construction process

- Develop confident staff who are inspired to contribute and make a difference

- To delight our clients with an honest and no surprises approach

- Senior involvement on all projects that sets us apart from the competition

- To be proactive and deliver on all promises, on time and to budget

- Upholding our reputation for reliability and quality

Next we turned to how to deliver the new strategy, the principal reason why Paul had asked me to come in. Rex Procter and Partners had for years been flatlining in sales in the West Yorkshire area that took in both Leeds and Bradford and the market itself had plunged since the credit crunch of 2008. The company's future depended on picking up customers and, especially, on opening up a new office in London, which was the one part of the building industry that had continued to hold up in Britain. This could never be achieved without the full commitment of the staff to the job in hand. So Paul and I started by analysing the strengths and weaknesses that could be found at RPP, involving everyone in the task of identifying just where our priorities must lie. We used a SWOT analysis.

The SWOT analysis is a well-known way of opening up discussion and identifying problems within the company. It gathers ideas and suggestions under four headings:

Strengths	Weaknesses
Opportunities	**Threats**

The SWOT analysis of RPP set against the strategy came up with 18 'action points'. These were allocated amongst the then senior partners who were asked to produce an action plan for each. This was a culture shock to most. The senior partners had never before been involved in such matters. Their job, as they saw it, was supervising the work of the

junior partners and gathering in the professional fees they had earned. Now we were asking the seniors to work ON as well as IN the business, a revelation for most. Paul took charge of making sure this was an initiative that was to be carried through to a conclusion. He told me: "These actions were reviewed by me personally on a monthly basis because in the past we had a culture of starting things but not finishing them. Not this time, I am determined to change our culture from one of complacency to one of performance."

This was a real challenge for Paul because both he and I felt people were waiting (and perhaps hoping) for this initiative to fail. But that was the point; it wasn't just any old initiative but a lifestyle change for the business. Paul was going to have to be persistent to see it through. The old 'way of doing things' was to be rooted out and the firm brought up to equal and surpass the very best. Take for example the new deal for the 'associate directors' who in the past may have been bored plodding through routine work.

"Through no fault of their own," Paul tells us, "the associate directors were not pulling their weight. Many of them would welcome a chance to show that things could be done differently, with fewer back-office staff and more individual responsibility for the job they were working on. Our surveys showed that the customers found the new service faster and more responsive and very competitively priced. In fact, on average, fee rates were down 30 percent from the peak of 2008, but the company continued to make profits."

Paul again. "We introduced regular staff briefings and management reviews of our progress. The best thing we did was to introduce David's idea of a weekly brain dump by all staff of customer snippets and intelligence they had gathered. We collected it together, joined the dots up and saw some real opportunities we never would have spotted previously."

In the course of 24 months the whole business was to be transformed from a rigid and hide-bound, white-collared professional service to become a modern, fast-moving service business. However, not everyone was pleased with the outcome. Paul had to break the bad news to the old style of worker; "Unfortunately, some people had to leave who could not

sign up to the new RPP way of doing business. We gave them a chance to change their ways to no avail," he told us. "So we took the opportunity to recruit some new high- quality people, including a marketing manager, for the first time, to promote our business. We opened a new office in London and started to court new clients. We invited up to 50 percent of our staff to become shareholders in our business and the results of our efforts over the past 2 years have given them a 6-fold return on their investments."

Now the two years are up, has it all worked? Paul Mackie gives a resounding yes. "We now have a presence in London and in nineteen market areas when previously we were only in eleven. We have a fantastic pipeline of new opportunities which we need to convert. Our culture has changed dramatically and we are in a much better place despite having been through the worst downturn in our industry I can ever remember. I have to pinch myself sometimes; we are now a business that is fit for the future rather than a dinosaur from the past and it's fantastic!"

But its roots have never been forgotten. Paul has emerged as a campaigner for the restoration of Bradford to its former glory. The 'Hole in the Ground' scheme will go ahead but under the close eye of Paul as vice-chairman of the Bradford Chamber of Commerce, the mistakes of the past seem unlikely to be repeated.

"If we had not engaged in the entrecode® revitalising process back in 2010 we would have gone bust by now."

This is a success story that could be emulated all over Britain now that the Entrepreneurial Code has been well and truly cracked. Not rocket science – it just works. However, not every business I tried to help revitalise using the **entrecode®** turned out to be a success. Take the case of Mr George.

The Story of Mr George – A Revitalisation Failure Story
Mr George's secretary Vanessa attended a seminar I ran in Leeds in April 2006. "Could you come and use your **entrecode®** stuff with my boss, he desperately needs help," implored Vanessa. So I travelled to Leeds

to meet with Mr George. He was a garment manufacturer making suits, raincoats and ladies shirts and dresses.

"I've read about this Entrecote work!" he bellowed.

"**entrecode®**," I corrected. "**entrecode®**."

"Well whatever!" he shouted even louder. "Young Vanessa said you could help me." This was the first clue to Mr George's character and it went downhill from there. Mr George turned out to be a third generation of a family business who had been well educated at an English public school. He had an air of superiority – looking down his nose at me and everybody else. I immediately knew we would not get on and should have walked after meeting him for five minutes but he intrigued me because he was idiosyncratic and passionate but clearly mad. Vanessa also was keen I should help so this is what happened:

Question one in revitalising a business is normally "what is your strategy?" This is then checked out by reviewing the past three year's financial records.

"Strategy, strategy, don't go for all that business tosh; we just make money here, that's our strategy."

Mr George's 'strategy' was not serving the business well as he had lost over £250k every year for the past three years. How had the business survived? Where did it get its funds from?

It turned out that his wife, who was the daughter of a very successful global engineering entrepreneur had 'invested' in his business.

"So what do you plan to do to get the business back on track?" I nervously enquired.

"Diversify, I've spotted an opportunity to buy a furniture business on the cheap, a little beauty".

So the strategy was to recover by taking his eye of his rapidly failing core business and get into one he knew absolutely nothing about. Also, if a business looks to be going too cheaply then the warning bells should be ringing. If it looks too good to be true it almost certainly is!

What about Mr George's team? His son Harry was the Sales Manager described by most people in the business as the Sales Prevention Officer. He apparently rarely visited the business only to take £100 out of the petty cash box without a receipt and to fill his car up at the company petrol pump. He was an arrogant young man, chip off the old block. His Finance Director was an elderly man aged 78 who was a book keeper who seemed to understand little about the accounts or finances generally. Honestly, you could not make this up

I decided to abandon my assignment when one day he announced a 10 percent pay cut for all staff and turned up in a brand new light blue Rolls Royce for himself. This was the last straw. Mr George's business reminded me of a rule that I had, which unfortunately I broke with him.

If it's not doable, don't do it! Never again.

On reflection I could not find one piece of the **entrecode**® in his business other than he was action oriented but not on the business! The problem I often face when asked to help revitalise a business is that the person who brings me in – the owner or CEO – turns out to be the problem. The issues are firstly, do you take on the job and if you do, how do you tell them; but more importantly, get paid! In 70 percent of cases when I confront the issue with them it is cathartic and they work hard at changing both themselves and their business. In thirty percent of cases I am asked to leave. As I told a new client recently "If you and I agree on everything one of us is not needed and that's almost certainly me!"

This is unsurprising since the fortunes of most businesses are directly linked to the personality, style and ability of the top person. One of the ways to take the pulse of whether a client and their business are really serious about revitalising the business is to create an actionometer. If we agree actions to be taken what percentage of them do they actually complete? Less than 50 percent is a good barometer that they are playing at it, 80 percent plus within the agreed timescales usually suggests that they intend to take it seriously and drive forward.

Interestingly, in the two cases in this chapter so far Paul Mackie and Rex Procter and Partners achieved 95 percent within the first 6 months and

Mr George….What do you think?

Actually, it was less than 10 percent.

The next challenge was to show how the **entrecode**® could be used to grow a successful business into a market leader.

Lessons Learned

- Businesses can be revitalised by following the **entrecode**® principles.

- Revitalisation requires the leadership to consistently drive the process and act as the role model for the changes required.

- You have to be persistent and get everybody on the bus and deal with those who are not prepared to make the journey.

- The most difficult thing to change in a business that requires revitalising is the culture.

- The starting point for change is re-do your strategy.

The entrecode® and Growing a Business the Keepmoat Way

Terry Bramall's story is testimony to what can be achieved by leaders who stay entrepreneurial throughout the life cycle of their business, resisting the temptation to becoming a rational steady state corporate manager.

It **was a dark** and moonless night in the early morning of 27th April 1942 when the sleeping citizens of York were awakened by the sound of exploding bombs. A German raiding party of some 40 bombers had slipped across the North Sea unchallenged, crossed the Humber at around a quarter-past-two, then turned west and descended to about 1,000 feet before releasing their deadly cargo on the historic centre of the city. The air-raid sirens failed to sound so bombs were already falling all around as the population, in night clothing, hurried to the nearest bomb shelter or cowered beneath kitchen tables. Ninety minutes later, the last plane passed overhead and headed off home.

Dawn brought a sober assessment of the wounds inflicted by the raid. York Minster survived some minor damage, but the historic Guildhall on the banks of the Ouse had been reduced to ashes. In Lavender Grove, close to the railway, an entire row of terraced houses had been all but flattened. Other streets were badly hit leaving 80 people across the City dead or mortally wounded – thankfully fewer than first reported.

Still, the raid left behind a major housing crisis. Once the city had been tidied up it was clear that 579 houses had been rendered completely uninhabitable and a further 2,500 damaged. Repairs were urgently needed but the skilled labour to do it was in short supply. York's disaster

presented an opportunity for neighbouring towns to come to the rescue, and in particular a firm of builders in Wath-upon-Derne (near Rotherham) called Bramall & Ogden.

George Bramall and Dick Ogden had got together to found the company in 1931. Their first contract had been for the local council, clearing out dry lavatories known as 'privy middens' at the back door of council properties and installing both indoor and outdoor flush toilets. But they could turn their hand to most jobs and they rose to the challenge of patching up York. And not just York. On another occasion they made a three-hundred-mile round trip to repair damaged homes in the badly hit city of Southampton.

It was a trying time for the Bramall & Ogden families, all close friends, for the work had to be carried out without any guarantee that the Luftwaffe would not return at any time. It had the habit of sending a second wave of bombers on the following night.

When the war came to an end, Bramall & Ogden may have anticipated a rebuilding boom but hopes for a big expansion in building jobs were soon dashed. Priority had to be given, instead, to repaying the debts owed to America under the wartime lend-lease scheme.

The business concentrated on building and refurbishing council houses at Wath- on-Dearne and schools, churches and small works. Their other pet project was to build up a bundle of small companies that would give them breadth of experience. One of them, Chantry Furniture, made carved pews for churches. But these 'hobby businesses' as I see them, had never made a profit. Terry Bramall, George's son, joined the business in 1968. By now the business had its own joiners and concrete shop and did their own haulage like all the local competitors. The business did quite well and made a profit during the early 70s. "I attended a local night class on bookkeeping which was the only help available but it was irrelevant; on reflection it was the last thing I should have done!" Terry Bramall now confesses.

It was a hard time for struggling building firms. Bramall & Ogden survived and picked up enough contracts to allow a modest growth in

business. They announced that as a general contractor they would build anything, anywhere, and at any price. It was a beguiling boast, but it hardly made business sense. In the immediate post-war years there was virtually no demand for 'bespoke building' of this sort. By the early 1970s the firm seemed bogged down, trying to do too much with too few resources and suffering from a 'jack-of-all-trades – master-of-none' syndrome. The company had a turnover of £25 million but was making a loss of £250,000 per year.

It was going nowhere. But then came a turning point. It began when Dick Ogden died in 1970 and the Bramall family bought out the Ogden interest. That was followed soon after by the appointment of Terry Bramall to the Bramall board, an important milestone in the search for profitability. Terry had opted to take a degree in civil engineering at Birmingham University before joining Taylor Woodrow where he met Dick Watson, a fellow engineering student, and they became good friends. In 1971 Terry invited Dick to join Bramall as a director. Terry and Dick formed a very lively partnership, determined to make the firm a major player in the local building scene.

"We managed the performance of our business through how much cash we had in the bank at the end of the month. We only knew how much profit we had made when we sat down with our accountant six months after the year end and thanked him as if he had made the money! Amazing when I look back." Terry Bramall told me at our first meeting.

This is when I was invited to help the business and the first job was to help them develop a clear business strategy. One of the outcomes of the early strategic thinking was they started by adopting the principle 'the easiest way to make money is to stop losing it'.

"It is a motto that every would-be successful entrepreneur should have pinned to his bedpost," recalls Terry. "When we applied it to the business it threw up some interesting results."

I should confess that, at this point, this survey of the company was one of the first jobs I did for Terry and Dick as a management consultant. There were many more to come. The same survey also revealed that three out

of the four senior managers were bringing in very poor results. On my recommendation they were asked to leave and find jobs somewhere else.

Refocusing the Business

The next challenge was to bring some focus into the business. Terry, Dick and I discussed this at length. Clearly spreading ourselves too thinly in a major market made no sense at all. But could we find a profitable niche from which we could, later, make our advance into big business territory? What were we really good at? Where were the profits to be made? I think we surprised ourselves to discover that our most profitable work was not in house building but in 'refurbishing' council-owned properties.

A large stock of council housing put up in the 1920s and 1930s, was in need of urgent attention to bring them up to the acceptable standards, while poor design and shoddy workmanship during the 60s and 70s meant that even fairly modern houses and flats were now being seen as a problem. To modernise these properties was not just a matter of retiling the roofs, sealing the windows, and applying a lick of paint. The kitchens and bathrooms needed replacing, central heating had to be put in, and communal gardens cried out for landscaping.

Bramall had spent years doing this sort of work and generally doing it well, but only really as a sideshow to the main business – small time house-building. Suddenly the scales slipped from their eyes. Here was a new market that Bramall was well placed to exploit. By concentrating our efforts on refurbishment and all that it entailed we would allow our workers to become the experts in the field. That was a real bonus. With my encouragement, they decided to seize the moment, opening what was to become a new chapter in the company's life.

To go with the change of tack the company desperately needed a new mission statement to guide it on the voyage. Terry, Dick and I argued over it for several months before producing the simple text that gave the business the focus it needed. Simple and unequivocal, it ran: **Bramall will become the market leader in refurbishing council houses in the North of England.**

Of course, there was the risk that we might fail to reach that goal, but it seemed a risk worth taking. For the new policy followed a well-trodden path taken by countless smallish companies determined to grow. Terry Bramall put it this way: "We decided to concentrate on what we knew we could do well and profitably. It's called 'sticking to the knitting' and this became Dick's mantra for the business." In my view it ought to be the golden rule for all growth businesses.

Armed with the new mission statement, Terry and Dick were raring to go. But one thing still stood in the way – Terry's love of the carpentry business. It troubled me, for the small joinery company had been haemorrhaging cash for years and there seemed no real prospect of turning it into a profitable asset. Take Chantry Furniture as one example. What kind of market was there for new church pews?

As a consultant, I spent considerable time trying to persuade Terry he must close the business down. But he resisted again and again, telling me, sometimes with a degree of irritation: "It will come good, I know it will. "Then, one day, he mentioned the pride his father had taken in building up the carpentry workshop. Suddenly I got it. To Terry this was an investment in nostalgia. To the rest of us it was a damaging distraction that swallowed up scarce resources and energy. He eventually accepted the logic of the argument and closed it down.

Building the Team

But the journey of transformation had only just begun. Terry and Dick recruited David Blunt as Finance Director. He had been selected to match our needs and was then subjected to a long interview and psychometric tests in which he had to convince us he was the man for the job. He joined Bramall in 1983 and proved a brilliant acquisition. It became clear during the strategic review that not all the directors shared the same vision of the future as Terry, Dick and David. Conflict of this kind can fatally damage a business. Some directors had to go.

The experience was difficult for all concerned, but it underlined the need for taking the matter of recruitment seriously. As it happened Terry had developed an understanding of his own strengths and weaknesses – a key

entrepreneurial skill. Henceforth, he surrounded himself with people who shared his values and had complementary skills to add to his own.

The same principles were to be extended to the recruitment of the workforce. Terry and Dick were looking for enthusiastic workers, with the necessary training, ready to put the customer, whether the council or the tenants, in pole position in their concerns. Anybody with experience of the old-style council bureaucracy will be aware that people in social housing don't always get treated as they should. So recruiting workers with the right social skills and the right attitude towards the customer would get our operation off to a flying start. The Mission Statement proved to be worth its weight in gold.

That is not to say that making money was our first priority. In our eyes it was the social purpose of the company that was also very important. Having a well-organised and dedicated workforce pleased the tenants and helped the councils themselves to change to a service ethos. It paid off in renewed contracts and a growing partnership with the councils. Bramall Construction could be trusted to do a good job and complete it on time, on cost. The word spread that it could solve the problems not just of the tenants but of the councils too.

Remember the entrepreneur's motto: seek a problem, solve a problem and see the opportunities roll in.

The Great Leap Forward
By 1983 Bramall Construction had built up a solid business from practically nothing. Now a new opportunity opened up, one that was to catapult the company into public notice. It began when Hogarth Shipping, the Glasgow shipbuilder, decided it should 'stick to the knitting' by disposing of non-core activities. Their diversification into social housing had proved a disaster. Their subsidiary company, Frank Haslam Milan (or FHM), required sorting out.

Unfortunately, Hogarth Shipping had neither the know-how nor *nous* to make a go of it. In 1983 they began a search for a corporate lifeboat to rescue the company from sinking. FHM had Doncaster connections and was engaged in the social housing market – building low cost homes

for low earners, often attracting a subsidy. In the eye of the FHM bosses, Bramall Construction must have seemed an ideal fit for a merger – the two companies did not exactly serve the same market but they had much in common. And FHM, being twice as large as Bramall Construction, might reasonably be expected to call the tune.

But when they approached Bramall Construction the canny Terry Bramall saw it very differently. While FHM had never made a profit, Bramall had achieved a turnover of £80 million and its profits had climbed steadily to reach over £1 million. Terry also had the advantage of knowing Hogarth Shipping was desperate to offload their FHM at almost any price. When it came to the actual negotiations Terry shrewdly took a back seat, convinced that the new financial director, David Blunt, would do a better job.

And that is how it worked out.

Brushing aside the suggestion of a merger on terms acceptable to the under-performing company, David suggested a price of £100,000 and a guarantee that Bramall would keep the jobs in FHM going. Take it or leave it. Hogarth Shipping had little alternative but to accept. It was game, set and match when David negotiated that all the FHM stocks in the warehouse should be handed over as part of the deal. While the ink on the agreement was still wet, Terry sent a message welcoming all the new staff to Britain's most ambitious new building company. That was the easy bit. Now he and his team had now to work out a strategy that would make the best use of both companies. They began with the new mission statement that simply ran:

"Delivering Community Regeneration"

This cleverly stressed the philosophy and purpose the companies would aim to share, as well as playing on their reputation of a company that delivered – often over delivered – on time. Of course, new house-building and the refurbishing of older properties were not the same, but the skills involved overlapped and Bramall Construction had direct experience of all aspects of house-building, from laying the foundations to fitting out the interior.

On the down side was the fact that, on average, most mergers have failed to bring any clear benefits to the predatory company. The odds against success are even greater when the taking-over firm is smaller than the one being taken over as it was in this case. It was a gamble, but one that Terry Bramall was confident he could win provided the new combined company could be run according to Bramall principles. The board gave him their enthusiastic support.

But what were these principles? Terry made sure that everyone would receive a briefing outlining what the business stood for. But that was only a beginning. To mark the transformation from being a smallish firm to a big player, he and the board began by giving the joint company a new name, one that everyone could be proud to belong to, whether they were working at Bramall or FHM. This name was Keepmoat – a name incidentally chosen at random from the Companies House store of names. It seemed to suggest strength and resolution.

With the new name came a new way to keep everyone well-informed about the image the new company would seek to present. Hewlett Packard in the USA had recently introduced what they called the HP Way as a means of building staff loyalty and giving clarity to its aims and philosophy. Using this as a template Keepmoat issued its own unique formula: **The Keepmoat Way.**

The Keepmoat Way (1986)

- Focus on regeneration of homes and building new starter homes

- Build partnerships with local authorities

- Delight customers

- Complete all jobs within cost and time deadlines

- Manage the milestones – key points on all contracts

- Induct people in the Keepmoat Way

- Use established processes to make good decisions and protect plans

- Treat each other with respect and dignity

- Encourage team working; particularly cross team

- Support managers through difficult trading times

As Terry explains: "This was not a useless piece of bureaucratic jargon, it was a statement in plain English of Keepmoat's objectives and its guiding principles. Because we had written them down, talked about them regularly and used them to help make decisions everybody appreciates what makes the company tick, what its values are. Obviously with time we might want to add or subtract from the recipe and everyone at Keepmoat was encouraged to raise issues they thought should be added or taken away. It was not cast in concrete."

Keepmoat indicated from the start that people could talk freely about the company and come up with their own ideas. But this was only a first step in what was to become a casebook study of how to integrate two disparate company cultures and meld them into one. A culture – by which I mean the values and behaviours of a company – is an asset for a company if it serves the business well; a liability if it is not. When one company takes over another there is almost certainly going to be a culture clash, a clash that has to be planned for and defused.

In the case of Keepmoat, it was anticipated that there could be resentment at the fact that the small fish had swallowed the big fish. There could also be a suspicion that the staff at Bramall Construction would be given favoured status by Terry and the directors when it came to promotion. So Terry, Dick Watson, and David Blunt made a point of travelling over to the FHM offices to meet the staff and discuss the future. The expedition worked a treat, especially since the directors were surprised at the quality of the managers and the junior staff. In the years that followed quite a number of the FHM employees were promoted to senior staff positions, both in Bramall Construction and at head office. The pep-talk from the directors was followed by a new training programme that everyone had to attend when invited.

Bramall had a long tradition of serious training, ever since the company had decided to go for the social housing market. This was when it was realised that a few ill-chosen words to a customer could destroy the very social model they were aiming to install – builders were not

particularly renowned for treating their customers (and especially their female customers) with the respect that was required. By the time of the Keepmoat merger, 20 odd years later, thanks to mentoring and group discussions, the builders' language and humour was much more restrained and their manner more professional.

But what Terry, Dick and David Blunt had in mind for the newly merged company was much more sweeping and revolutionary than anything before attempted in the building and associated trade, as far as I can tell. They wanted to embed a common company culture in the psyche and hearts of everyone involved in the company from the highest to the lowest. As I have written previously: 'Culture is an asset if it serves the business, but a liability if it does not … Companies get their culture by design, sometimes, more often by default, which is usually one they don't want!"

The Keepmoat Way was a start but only a start. Company strategy and company culture ought to go hand in hand. In Terry's words: "Strategy is WHAT, Culture is HOW"; both can be equally important.

Creating a Preferred Culture

The Keepmoat policy regarding culture was to 'embed it' in everything the company did and in every individual who worked for the company. This meant investing in training to make sure everyone understood the importance not only of the hard skills but of the soft skills, the people skills that gave Keepmoat a competitive advantage, especially in capturing the hearts of the customer and winning the approval of the council staff they had to work with. It was an essential process since the customer delight experienced by the councils and tenants would feed back this to their officers and so influence future contracts.

Naturally, the training in delighting customers aroused an initial scepticism. David Blunt tells how the macho males among both sets of staff raised eyebrows when the subject was first introduced in the training room: "It was counter cultural," he says. The attitude was 'This is not what industry does'" But the company took a different view and used feedback from customers to make it clear that customer-friendly behaviour from now on would be the norm.

Strategy

While the cultural questions were being sorted out Terry and his team were hard at work on the other half of the equation – getting the strategy right. It was agreed there should be a strategy review each year to assess how the businesses should react to changing circumstances.

For the first time Keepmoat looked beyond its 'home' territory and decided to open offices in Newcastle and Manchester. But it proved to be a stiffer task than the board had anticipated. Both were led by managers who lived locally and who had worked with council contracts. The problem was that the Keepmoat Way was not fully understood by the new people. Eventually they were replaced by experienced managers from Keepmoat's head office in Mexborough, near Doncaster.

Sorting out this problem had to be done against a background of a new target for the business, doubled to £100 million sales a year. Only when both offices turned in a good profit after five years and went on to do very well, did those at head office relax. It was seen as a lesson to be learned, and it was.

In 1999 Keepmoat clocked up sales of £100 million. In light of the performances of the original business and of the new acquisition, the board went for a strategy of expansion not least because more public money would have to be pumped into housing to meet the targets set in the *Decent Homes* Initiative. The White Paper of 2001 pledged the government to bring all social housing up to a decent standard by 2010. This would mean a big increase in the budget for refurbishing older properties and for making sure any new social homes met an improved standard.

Visioning

In the light of these opportunities various ideas were tried to see how the quality of our management could be improved. One of these was a new technique called visioning, one very popular in America but virtually unknown here. It aims to introduce entrepreneurial thinking into the management process. Managers were encouraged to create a vision for their part of the business and then prepare and deliver plans to achieve

that vision. The exercise raised the spirits of the business at a time when trade was bad. But it also resulted in a surge in sales. At first there was no parallel increase in profits, but that was because the competition out there was very stiff.

Keepmoat now tried a more radical tack. Instead of going through the exercise in what had been an abstract manner, we asked the managers to take it further, imagining they were entrepreneurs and this time focusing on action plans to improve their profits. The 'every person a business person' initiative. Astonishingly, the exercise showed improvements in notional 'profits'. Even more remarkably their units then improved their real profits.

The Ten Million Team and The Big Hairy Audacious Goal

The 'ten million pound team' was set up. The thinking behind it was to ask our most entrepreneurial senior people to conduct an audit of the companies to see how a further £10 million might be saved. The team established that really big opportunities to reduce costs were to be found in plenty. They also established that three quarters of Keepmoat's costs went on purchasing building materials and paying contractors. That was an eye-opener.

The Importance of Buying

Keepmoat was a great business to be associated with. As a consultant I could throw in ideas and see many of them implemented. Sometimes they came up trumps. Take for example the remarkable benefit from a visit we had from a buyer of Walmart. He gave a talk on buying. Not so much a talk as a discussion and demonstration. He asked one of our ten young managers to demonstrate an imaginary buying session. When the demonstration was finished the buyer shook his head. "Your system is that you buy anything from anywhere, at any price, at any time. That was how we did it twenty years ago. Let me show you how we do it now."

At the end of the session I asked our guest how much his methods would save us on costs. "Around 15 to 20 percent," he said. The whole room went quiet.

"Wow" said David Blunt, "With a reduction in buying costs on that scale we would increase our profits by a factor of three."

Thanking our guest we went back to the office and started drawing up a new policy on buying in building materials. At a fair estimate, it would reduce Keepmoat's buying costs by £100 million over a ten-year period.

The greatest triumph, though, arose out of an idea flagged up in an American business book. It was the year 2000 and the book was *Good to Great*, the work of Jim Collins. In it he argued that people were held back by a failure of imagination when it came to running a business. The most successful business people thought big and did not allow criticism or a sudden failure of nerve to put them off. He suggested people could overcome their inhibitions when it came to thinking big by creating a Big Hairy Audacious Goal (BHAG) and imagining it was by your side.

Terry Bramall was struck by the idea. It could be used to make people at Keepmoat think big too, to the benefit of the company and the staff. The top Keepmoat team were issued with copies and a long discussion led by Dick Watson ensued as to whether there was something to be said for the idea. It inspired them to refocus their business dramatically. **The new aim was to become a billion pound business within the next ten years, with a profit of £100m.**

It was thinking big in a big way.

But just how was this ambition to be achieved? At board level, there was agreement that as a company we had to get smarter from the foundations to the roof. We had to start thinking like a billion pound business. We had already had coaching and mentoring support to keep ideas fresh and techniques up to the minute. But it could not deliver the quantum leap we all felt was needed. Out of the discussion came the Keepmoat Academy. Its aim was to train managers how to run a billion pound business. The top team attended a leadership programme at Ashridge Management College, set in wooded country outside London and regarded as one of the best of its kind. Up and coming managers were signed up for a Master of Business Administration course run at Keepmoat by the staff of Nottingham Business School. Over 50 of them

successfully completed the course and were each slotted back into the company. Career planning was set up to give every employee a chance to discuss the future prospects. It was an extraordinary programme that continued as the various off-shoots of Keepmoat were launched and turned into a profit.

In all the businesses the customer remained king. Supporting the community remained a cornerstone, with the company sponsoring community events and apprenticeship schemes expanded and improved to bind the company and its clients ever more closely together. The whole edifice was supported and motivated by a bi-monthly magazine aimed at both staff and customers. The message loud and clear was that this is a company that's going places.

Up until 2007 the targets were met. Even the recession, which struck the building industry so hard in 2008, did little to dent the optimism or the performance. But Terry Bramall and Dick Watson were nearing retirement age. David Blunt stood ready to take over, heading a sale that valued the business at nearly £767 million. The rest is history.

The business was eventually sold for £783 million to HBOS. The ink had no sooner dried on the agreement when the Bank of Scotland had to be rescued by an emergency loan and the deal with Keepmoat thrown off course. To start rebuilding the bank, the owners (you and I) put Keepmoat up for sale to the highest bidder. It was bought by Coller Capital for a knockdown price of £400m along with 39 other HBOS businesses. During the period 2005-2011 Keepmoat produced industry-leading profits of over 10 percent every year whilst the nearest competitors averaged 4 percent! This was a magnificent achievement by the Keepmoat management team.

The years of constantly working on the business and refreshing the entrepreneurial spirit paid off handsomely. However, in 2012 the new owners merged Keepmoat with Apollo, another of the portfolio they had acquired.

Will the Keepmoat way, based upon family business values and taking a long- term view, survive the change into a large corporate business run by venture capitalists? Let's hope so. I wish it well, but mourn the loss of family control of one of the most remarkable building companies to have emerged since the Second World War.

Lessons Learned

- Following the **entrecode**® principles it is possible to build a business with industry-leading market share, profits and reputation.

- A clear focused strategy should be the touchstone for all business decisions and activity.

- Competitive advantage can be gained by designing a culture that serves the business.

- Get the right people on the team with shared values and complementary skills.

- The easiest way to make money is to stop losing it.

- Treating all stakeholders with dignity and respect creates pride, commitment and people willing to produce results beyond expectations.

- Ensure you are constantly working 'on' as well as 'in' the business.

Chapter Thirteen

Innovate or Die – Get Better or Get Beaten

The unlocking of the key to the entrepreneur mindset has transformed companies such as Paul Mackie's RPP, fundamentally changing the company culture and opening the way to real and sustained growth. But as companies grow and take on more staff, it is vital to find a way to maintain that momentum. That is where innovation comes in. As the speed of the business cycle has gathered pace the need for continuous innovation becomes more and more urgent. In the high tech world of the tablet computer and the smartphone there needs to be a constant flow of new high quality products or services in the pipeline if the enterprise is to continue and flourish. It's all too easy to trip up at this stage – as the stories of Nokia and Blackberry show only too clearly. So where does the entrepreneur stand in this fast moving world?

In 2006 I decided to investigate the problem of innovation and came across a survey of large corporations conducted for the Harvard Business Review on the question of innovation. It revealed what I call the innovation paradox. For 90 percent of the senior executives polled, innovation was one of their key priorities. But the same survey found the same 90 percent confessed it had proved all but impossible to achieve the targets they had set themselves.

There are clues as to why this should be. A total of 95 percent of all 'radical innovations' in business was created by small entrepreneurial firms (source: *New Venture Creation, Prof. J A Timmons*). Another study found that small firms produced 24 times as many innovations per head as large firms. The small firms seemed to hold the key to generating the much needed innovation. This was especially true of the hi-tech sector. So it's no

surprise that a big corporation like Proctor and Gamble – involved in food processing and detergents for the consumer market – has adopted a policy of buying in half of its innovative ideas from small companies.

It is rather sad to think that companies that were once at the forefront of innovation now seem to have lost their way. So can we restore innovation to its pride of place in the struggle for business survival in these difficult times?

One revelation that emerged from the deciphering of the Entrepreneurial code is the exciting discovery that entrepreneurs can be developed as well as bred. It means that companies, who have long lost touch with their spirit of innovation, can regenerate through tapping into the talents of their people using the **entrecode**® processes. How can it be done? Let's begin by looking at an example of the man behind Britain's best hope of leading the world in internet technology, an opportunity that was allowed to slip away.

In 1963 Ajaz Ahmed was born into a poor Pakistani family in Lahore, Pakistan. When he was three, his father – in search of a better life – brought the family to Huddersfield where he took employment in a local textile mill. Ajaz and the family grew up in a cramped and crumbling terrace house with not even an indoor toilet. At school he did badly, leaving at the age of 16 with no qualifications. But eventually he was taken on as a shop assistant in the Huddersfield branch of the big electrical retailer, Dixons. He enjoyed the job and it showed. He progressed through the company training scheme and moved smoothly up the management ladder to become a store manager.

Then, in the early 90s, he was bitten by the computing bug and looked for a new challenge. When Dixons acquired PC World, then a small company specialising in computing, he applied for a transfer and was duly appointed store manager of the new PC World in Leeds, the first to be opened in the north of England. It proved a good move. In 1995 only one percent of households in Britain owned a computer. Computers were generally seen as business tools, a sort of glorified typewriter that could do sums and keep a tag on the accounts. It was a machine beloved by so-called 'techies', far beyond the understanding of the common man.

But all that was about to change as the Internet was about to arrive. It would not only open the way to masses of instant information but also introduce the concept of 'emailing' and to stay at home digital shopping of the sort promised by Amazon. As a store manager surrounded by computers and digital gadgets, Ajaz was well positioned to explore the new digital age. In 1996 he bought his first internet-ready computer. But when he tried to get on the Net he found it was not as easy as he imagined – in fact it was cumbersome and very slow. He turned for help to his staff in the store but they had no idea how it could be done. There was nothing for it but to do some research in the pages of a specialist computing magazine. With the magazine came a CD from Compuserve that promised to link the computer to the digital network in return for a subscription and a charge for every session spent on the Net.

He loaded the CD and, following the instructions, managed at last to get on to the internet. "I thought, wow, this is fantastic, this is the future, and everybody should have access to this. This was my Eureka moment. I saw immediately that if we could provide a CD like this for our customers and control the front page, then that would give us access to them with very low marketing costs, as we wouldn't have to advertise."

Ajaz took his idea to his managing director who unfortunately didn't understand it and told him to forget it. Ajaz takes up the story: "I nearly gave up after that. I came across an article in *Vanity Fair* about the new establishment and the old establishment, the old establishment being oil and steel barons and the new establishment being computer and media people. There was a quote from Ted Turner, who was the owner of CNN and the first man to start the 24-hour news channel. At the time 24-hour news must have seemed a stupid idea to most people but now everyone uses it.

Turner's advice to entrepreneurs was "**Do the obvious before it becomes obvious to everybody else.**" "This was a second Eureka moment for me," Ajaz says, "because, if we acted quickly, we could give access to the internet before anyone else."

Fortunately, the director, who originally rejected the idea, had now left the company. It provided an opportunity for Ajaz to take his idea to the

group's chief executive. He listened carefully and then said, "Let's do it." But he added a warning; "Don't spend too much money."

"We eventually spent £240K which is not a bad return in creating a £1.5 billion business," says Ajaz. Some would have been dismayed at this less than encouraging remark but Ajaz left the meeting determined to show the company that it really could be done without any great investment. He saw it as a challenge and rose to meet it. He duly surprised the top management by coming up with a workable plan of action.

Freeserve was launched on 22nd September 1999. After an announcement on the One O'clock News, people were soon queuing at the stores to get their Freeserve CDs. Within three months it became the largest ISP provider in the country and within nine months it was floated on the stock market for an astonishing £1.5 billion. Then the dot.com boom lifted its value fleetingly to £9 billion, which was more than that of its parent company, the Dixon Group. Eventually the business was sold two years later for £1.6 billion to France Telecom. By this time Ajaz had moved on to further entrepreneurial projects.

The lessons according to Ajaz from this spectacular story of entrepreneurial growth are:

- Be prepared to do the obvious before everybody else.
- Find a customer problem and solve it by looking at it from the customer's perspective.
- Make it really easy for customers to buy from you.

"If entrepreneurs just applied these principles, many more could be as successful as Freeserve was," say Ajaz.

He left with a fair amount of cash in his pocket. He still lives in Huddersfield and takes a close interest in business. He has been associated with a number of online start-ups, including Browzar, a browser that allows people surf the web, without leaving a trace of their digital footprints. More recently he's been part of a group setting up a new Internet Legal Service www.legal365.com which will loosen the grip of lawyers and speed up the legal process. As a low-cost provider it could be a winner.

"Most people," reckons Ajaz, "will come up with at least one world-class idea in their lives. But the sad thing is that most people won't do anything about it." Talking to him, it seems to me that nothing frustrates him more than seeing good business ideas go unexploited.

So what advice would he give anyone contemplating starting their own company? "Talk to someone about the idea," he says. He continues: "There are lots of people who will help you; other successful entrepreneurs are a good place to go first."

Ajaz also points out that it's easy to get good feedback from people who know you. But their opinions don't really count. "It's vitally important to get feedback from potential customers," he advises. "Your idea will live or die by your customers' reaction. I imagine myself in a busy high street, asking people if they'd use this product or service. Trying to get a customer's perspective is very important."

And the economy? "Don't use the recession as an excuse not to start a business," he continues, "in some ways, a recession is a good time; you generally have lower costs, and it's easier to find staff."

Ajaz engaged in 'purposeful practice' even before he got his first management role at Dixons. "I read every business book I could lay my hands on as well as business magazines and the *Financial Times*. I became a swot. So when I moved into my first management job I hit the deck running because I had developed a management mindset. I simply put into practice the ideas I had studied." This resonates very much with the 'apprenticeship' I served when preparing myself to become a management consultant, but the 'purposeful practice' both Ajaz and I had applied to our studies served us both well.

I really liked Ajaz when I first met him July 2000. He had been amazingly successful but he seemed to be a very normal, unassuming guy, articulate and very friendly and open about sharing his experiences, both successes and learnings. No ego, flash cars or apparent need to impress. Just an ordinary guy in many ways, but one with a burning desire to succeed and a belief in himself.

The Ajaz story demonstrates the potential for innovation in large organisations when an entrepreneur takes the responsibility for creating something new. So lesson one is to find the entrepreneur within your organisation and encourage them to do what they do best – innovate. However, in many organisations there is a major problem which prevents innovation occurring. Our research discovered that the prevailing culture is the major reason why 90 percent of existing organisations are unable to innovate. It is a culture that concentrates power at the top, from where it passes down through the ranks to those at the bottom who are expected to do as they are told. It can be described as a power and control culture with a focus on:

- Job descriptions
- Organisation charts
- Rules and procedures
- Budgets
- Business plans
- Formal Meetings

We found that this culture seriously inhibits innovation.

In the case of Ajaz we have seen how one person can spot a superior opportunity and by persistence drive it through despite the power and control culture. But in many of the large companies there is either a dearth of talent – which I doubt – or no means of identifying and liberating it.

What would happen, I thought, if we could find someone in the company with entrepreneurial skills and try a different approach?

Ajaz has issued a challenge to corporate CEOs. "If somebody in your organisation came to you with an idea would you turn them away? People are running businesses who have never worked at the sharp end with customers so how do they really know a good idea that customers would be interested in? In difficult times it is critical that all the good ideas are encouraged and used – it's common sense," says Ajaz.

How Not To Innovate

I undertook a project back in the mid-90s in one of the leading UK blue chip chemical businesses in the North East of England. They had dozens of Phd Chemists working earnestly in labs but the business was in terminal decline because it could not innovate. Their process for innovating was to gather nominated people in a room and tell them they needed to innovate. The team met usually on a Friday afternoon, attendance at the meetings was at best sporadic. The team had S.M.A.R.T. objectives, a secretary took minutes and action plans by the team were produced yet nothing happened. Nobody took responsibility for doing anything but the process gave the illusion of progress.

Mistake One

Selection of team members. The attendees were nominated and were probably good at what they do but were not entrepreneurs. They did not think in a creative, entrepreneurial manner.

Mistake Two

Meeting on a Friday afternoon, end of the week when people are tired and wanted to go home…not smart.

Mistake Three

Giving a team S.M.A.R.T. objectives is a bureaucratic management process that limits innovation because it can set the sights too low and it takes the focus away from the creative, intuitive process.

Mistake Four

Producing action plans. Entrepreneurs take action; they do not produce plans which don't get implemented.

Mistake Five

There was no culture of people taking responsibility for taking action and nobody was held to account. Action taking in entrepreneurial businesses is non-negotiable, not by force but by people taking personal ownership.

Mistake Six

Setting up weekly innovation meetings is a mistake because it's a routine which left-brain businesses adopt. If innovation is that important it should take priority.

Innovation cannot survive in a power and control culture. The culture squeezes the life blood out of the creative process and people.

Back in 2001 I discovered an unexpected fact that 95 percent of all the innovations in the past 100 years in products and services worldwide had come from firms employing less than 20 people! I found this an amazing statistic because it's counter-intuitive. I would expect large firms to be able to innovate because they have smart people, resources, finance and networks, yet they cannot innovate. Why?

So what lay behind it? Research has shown, it is a product of typical corporate management. Power is concentrated at the top and the way of thinking is constrained by rules and procedures. These often act as an 'energy vampire', sucking the energy out of the business. We thought there must be something in this so we researched the culture in small innovative organisations. We found it marked by a different type of culture where people were producing results, often way beyond expectations, with the focus on achievement, where people were encouraged to:

- Just do it!
- Run trial and error pilots
- Seek forgiveness not permission
- Break the rules
- Work at pace

Their cultures were 180 degrees different from large power and control organisations. So we started to experiment in large organisations by finding the entrepreneurs within and then creating an achievement culture and the results were outstanding, by a factor of six. We called this the entrepreneurial premium. Let's have a look at a business which has managed to create a culture of innovation over many years.

Gripple And Innovation

You'll remember Hugh Facey; we met him in Chapter Two where he described how he started his business. Hugh was a Sheffield Wire Fencing manufacturer, had spotted a superior opportunity when he heard the story of farmers struggling to repair their barbed wire fences. It sparked the ideas of the 'Gripple', a cleverly designed wire fastening and tensioning system that could repair fences in an instant and put an end to torn hands. He spent three years developing the idea before launching it on the farming community. It was a hit from day one, and orders began piling in – including a contract to supply Gripples to secure the longest fence in the world, the famous Australian Dingo Fence.

But for all this success Hugh was not one to relax and think the good times would last forever. All good ideas have their shelf life. And even 20-year patents – of which Hugh and his company have many – eventually expire. Hugh firmly believes that only a steady programme of innovation can keep the company on its toes and in rude health. As he told a Sheffield reporter: "Innovation is so much more than a simple buzzword; it's the foundation of our culture." He was one of the first to put 'ideas and innovation' at the top of the company agenda. There was a logic behind it that is hard to challenge. No company, he told me, should be happy to dish up the same old product year after year. In a highly competitive market it is a question of innovate or perish. If you don't change you'll be overtaken by rival firms who will seek to copy what you're doing and improve on it.

There are three ways of dealing with the problem. Firstly, you can take out patents to protect your intellectual property for a 20-year period. That's helpful but without new products or services to offer the customers you'll face erosion of your competiveness in the long-run. Secondly, you can exploit new markets overseas, both in Europe and America, where the market is a lot larger – but you must centre your operations in places that make sense. Lastly, you need to create an environment in which new ideas and innovations can be born and flourish.

Hugh has adopted all three strategies to brilliant effect justifying his faith in foreign markets by selling more than 85 percent of his product abroad.

"As I see it," he told me, "Britain represents only 5 percent of the world market, which means that 95 percent of world markets are open to my products."

It may be a rough and ready index of opportunity but it seems to work. However, it is the flow of ideas that presents the greatest challenge. His big idea has been to create an 'innovation department' in one of his Sheffield factories. It is staffed by 12 people. Every time someone has an idea that is worth pursuing – that's left to them to decide – they sound a claxon.

Hugh defends it as "just a bit of fun that creates some energy among the staff". But it's working, according to Mark Edmunds the Managing Director in charge of innovation. "Within the ideas and innovations team we don't have people in charge. The same goes for the people who make the Gripple. Everyone is open-minded. We are free spirits, free from regulation and job titles, and very team-oriented."

None of them has much of a job description. Amazingly it seems to work. The teams, who are multi-skilled, decide who will do what on any particular day.

Hugh believes it's a winning combination: "We've kept that culture going over the last 20 years. We started off with just three people and have grown to 5 and then 10, and now 350, but the team spirit has always stayed the same."

But the pressure to innovate and improve will always be there. To make sure they never lose sight of the need to innovate a target has been set of a quarter of the sales in any year should be of products and services introduced within the previous four years. So far this has worked well, keeping the sales staff focused, and the Ideas and Innovations Department on their toes.

Underpinning the whole approach is a unique strategy to bring in new customers and keeping them on-side. It's **the problem-seeking, problem-solving** approach highlighted in Chapter Two.

The sales force is a critical element here. They meet customers regularly and discuss progress and any difficulties that have arisen. They go armed

with a promise 'send us your problem and we'll see if our design team can offer you a solution'. We never say NO to a challenge.

The fruits of this policy were soon to be seen. When the London Gherkin was going up, the Gripple sales team met the architects and convinced them that Gripple hanging units could replace many of the costly metal air conditioning suspension units. As a result, 9,000 Gripple Units and 18,000 patented 'corner saddles' were fitted in the services areas. They are never seen by the public but play a vital role in making this iconic building a great place to work.

And the fashion caught on. Gripple wires and hangers have proved amazingly successful in winning contracts for the big American sports stadia. Dallas Cowboys' new stadium has a remarkable spiral duct venting stale air into the atmosphere – Gripple 'Hangers' hold the separate elements together, allowing over 100,000 fans to watch the spectacle in total ignorance of what lies above.

The rise of the Gripple and its ancillary parts have provided a much cheaper and easier way to install essential services ducting, saving millions and sparing the planet all the energy that would have been used using conventional methods. As the company puts it modestly 'by replacing traditional threaded rod installations with Gripple hangers, steel consumption is reduced by 95 percent'.

The popularity of the Gripple was celebrated by Hugh and his team when Europe's tallest building, the Shard opened for business in 2012. It stands at over a thousand feet, and had 87 floors including Europe's highest restaurant. Inside the glass skin hundreds of thousands of Gripples and Gripple hangers help keep the place comfortable, whatever the weather, day and night.

But, while expansion of the business across the world is in full stream with company offices in Chicago, New Delhi, Alsace, Baden-Baden and Sao Paulo, we mustn't forget Britain. The innovation team in Sheffield has come up with some remarkable ideas, ideas that seem to bear little family resemblance to the Gripple or its spin-offs. The subsidiary company set up to manufacture this new range of attractions is called Loadhog which hints at the purpose of this offshoot from the Gripple stable.

The business caters for what is now popularly known as "Logistics", everything to do with moving loads and interfacing with road haulage. It bears many of the hallmarks of the Gripple approach, including the same challenge to customers. It proclaims "We're committed to introducing new, patented products designed with the express purpose of solving problems."

The Pallets, the Hog Box, the Pally, and the Pally Magnum are all made of lightweight materials that are waterproof and much lighter than conventional paleting systems. The primary attraction of these units is that they cut out the need for plastic wrapping and help manufacturers meet new targets in reducing land-fill and recycling. Loadhog boasts: "For one customer in the retail market the Hog Box will save annually the equivalent of 68 Olympic- sized swimming pools (6,000 tonnes) of packaging waste, and halve the number of vehicle journeys required. It eliminates the need for pallets.

The *piece de resistance* is a new pallet design for carrying empty bottles to breweries or glassworks vastly reducing breakages. The system is one of the fruits of the innovation strategy and has already secured a healthy share of the pallets and packaging market.

Hugh has reached retiring age but will never retire unless forced out by the shareholders. That seems unlikely since he has long-championed the cause of employee ownership. Taking up shares in the company after a year has become a pre-condition for all wishing to work at Gripple. Under the present arrangement would-be employees have to buy 1000 shares at the end of their first year. "It's the best system we could have," says Hugh. "It makes for a happier and well-integrated workforce and helps improve our efficiency at all levels within the company. There is, I am pleased to say, no 'them' and 'us' attitudes here."

That policy is reflected in the way Gripple has created industrial premises that have caught the imagination in the industrial heart of Sheffield. The Old West Gun Works and the new Riverside building have been joined by the Hog Works, once a grimy wreck of a place, now lovingly restored to house the Loadhog business. All three measure up to the highest

standards, as good as the best hi-tech factories to be found anywhere in the world.

They represent Hugh's mission to keep manufacturing jobs in Britain. Once you have the protection of the patent, he told me, you can invest in having the main manufacturing base here, not in the Far East. "Our policy is to make our Gripples and Hangers here in Sheffield using the latest technology. The same is true of Loadhog. It has taken years to develop both businesses but we are reaping the rewards now and will continue to reap them."

Hugh believes it is only by constantly ploughing money back into the business that they can keep abreast of the competition. But this business, founded only in 1998, has another reason to be cheerful. Because it is employee-owned it is virtually guaranteed not to be the target of some 'get rich quick' takeover bid of the kind that has so undermined British business.

As Hugh says, "I won't be leaving right away, but Gripple and Loadhog will go from strength to strength."

Lessons Learned

- Existing organisations can innovate providing they engage their entrepreneurs and create an achievement culture.
- The entrepreneurial approach of problem seeking, problem-solving is the heart of the innovation process.
- Encourage innovation through low cost/low risk pilots.
- Ensure the power and control culture does not inhibit risk taking and innovation.
- Banish the 'energy vampires'.
- Persistence is key to successful innovation.

Chapter Fourteen
An Entrepreneur with a Noble Purpose

My definition of entrepreneurship is creating value from practically nothing. However, value is no always about making money. It can be about creating value in people's lives, the community, or society as a whole. Dr Fiona Wood's remarkable story is an example of an entrepreneur with a noble purpose.

Nobody expected it. That evening in the Kuta Beach area of Bali the nightclubs were packed with young Australians, many just off the plane, set on making this a holiday to remember. The resort was famous for its relaxed beaches and its vibrant nightlife. It was the south-west Pacific equivalent of Ibiza or Ajja Napa, attracting millions of tourists every year.

On this October evening, as the clock crept steadily towards midnight, the holidaymakers were too focused on the evening ahead to notice a Mitsubishi van parked outside the Sari nightclub. Meanwhile, only yards up the road, a second nightclub, Paddy's, was already bulging at the seams. There, a young man carrying a rucksack on his back paused for a moment to check his watch and then pushed his way into the club. Before anyone could challenge him, he detonated his device.

All hell let loose. There was a rush out into the street where, only seconds later, the second, much larger bomb was detonated outside the Sari Club, leaving a wall of flames illuminating the tangled wreck of the van and a great hole in the ground with mangled bodies scattered around it. The whole scene was, as one eyewitness described it, "hell on earth". Just how devastating the bomb attack had been in terms of human lives and

suffering slowly became apparent. The death toll came to a staggering 202, of whom 88 were Australian. However, as well as the dead there were 240 casualties, many of them severely burnt and in a critical state.

The local hospital could not handle the disaster, and an urgent call went out for medical help. The nearest big hospital was in Perth, the capital of Western Australia, fully 1600 miles away. Fortunately, the hospital, the Royal Perth, had anticipated that some day a major disaster like this might occur and had drawn up an emergency plan. As a result, all of the seriously ill survivors were flown back to Australia within a day and a half, most of them directly to Perth.

The woman in charge in Perth, and the driving force behind the emergency plan, was then Western Australia's only female plastic surgeon, an extraordinary woman called Fiona Wood. The operation was not only a success because of its speed, but the survival rate of patients suffering from severe burns was far higher than expected.

As head of the Burns Unit, Fiona had spent years treating patients with severe injuries and knew just how terrible it was to see patients coming in apparently full of life, only for complications to set in and for death to follow, despite all efforts to save them. It was a bitter experience for the dedicated staff to come to terms with.

However, in Perth, many of those expected to die survived. In the case of patients who had lost up to 75 percent of their skin, not one died. Among those with more than 90 percent loss of skin – normally regarded as impossible to save – only half didn't make it.

This was the miracle of Bali.

For her achievements in treating the victims of the Bali bombing, coordinating a team of 60 doctors and nurses and minimising the loss of life, Fiona was honoured in 2005 by being named Australian of the Year. So how can we account for her success? We will find it can largely be explained by one factor, Fiona was an entrepreneur.

Today, Fiona Wood is an Aussie through and through, but she was born in England in 1958, the daughter of a coalminer and a school matron. Well, this final fact is not quite true. Indeed, her mother was a youth worker

until Fiona was 13. Fiona takes up the story: "There was a school close to the village where we lived and the girls wore this fabulous uniform, a bit like Harry Potter. It was a Quaker school and I desperately wanted to go there but it was a private school and my parents couldn't possibly find the fees. But my mother knew that daughters of staff members got in for free. She saw there was a vacancy for a school matron so she applied and got an interview. I don't quite know how she swung it but she emerged as the school's new PE teacher. My place was assured."

There was a strong sense of community and intellectual curiosity in the mining village culture that Fiona grew up in. The motto of Ackworth School, which she was so desperate to attend, was "*Non Sibi Sed Omnibus*" ("Not for One's Self but for Others"), which deeply influenced her to engage in the community and help others.

Fiona loved maths and science but her parents and elder brother were adamant she should study medicine. Her exam marks were excellent and she secured a student post in one of London's best hospitals, St Thomas's, just across the Thames from the Houses of Parliament. She did particularly well, earning first class honours and subsequently winning a place in the medical school, one of only twelve women in that 1975 intake.

After a year, she faced the first whiff of sexism and showed her mettle: "I had to decide which specialism I should follow and I chose surgery. At that time it was very much a male preserve. I think that a number of people didn't consider it appropriate that I should pursue a surgical career, but I didn't consider it appropriate that they should tell me. I'd sort of ignore that. My standard line was: 'I'm really good at embroidery so just watch out.'"

In 1986, this feisty woman made a move that was to change her life. She got married to an Australian surgeon studying in London, and he made it a condition that she should go to live with him in Perth. It disappointed her mother when she found her daughter had agreed to go to Perth, Australia, and not the much more accessible Perth, Scotland.

But when she arrived, Fiona soon settled down, dazzled by the sunny climate and the way of life far removed from the frozen north of England.

She was eventually to have six children, and between births Fiona completed her exams as a surgeon and chose the specialism of burns surgery. Fiona later revealed her reasons for making the choice: "Surgery, for me, was a no-brainer. I was very excited and interested by anatomy – which may sound strange, but it was one of those things that I really was interested in. And the obvious place to go from anatomy was into surgery. I simply thought, 'It's not a question of *whether* I'll be a surgeon, it's just where and when.'"

In part, it was also because she had a fascination with the challenge of dealing with severe burns. Up to then, it had been an area of medicine where disappointment and hurt were commonplace. Fiona sees this every day: "People ask me, 'Why do you keep going?' And I think, well, because one day we'll be able to do this such that we can reduce that suffering all the time. Reduce it, reduce it and one day maybe we will be able to do it without a whole heap of this suffering happening. And so that's the motivation to keep going."

Fiona spent years working in the burns unit at the Royal Perth, steadily acquiring experience, but without realising how close she was to vindicating her faith that the treatment of burns could be revolutionised. In 1991, she was appointed head of the Burns Service Unit at Royal Perth, which included the children's unit at the Princess Margaret Hospital for Children. She now had more freedom to begin the search for a solution to the difficult challenge of the high mortality rate associated with severe burns.

In 1993, the paths of Fiona and her future collaborator in the realm of medical science crossed when she met Marie Stoner, then a junior medical researcher. Marie and Fiona happened to meet socially at the hospital and got to talking about the developing science of skin replacement. American scientists had found a way to put a small piece of skin in a Petri dish (a flat, shallow container designed to grow cultures) and grow it into a sizeable sheet. This could be spread across the patient's burnt area – after carefully cleaning it – and left to grow. Provided the new skin was genetically identically to that of the burns patient, it ought to take.

But Fiona found it was a difficult trick to pull off. The skin often developed with holes in it, and the length of time required to grow the new skin risked complications such as deadly infections and organ failure. Marie, it turned out, had been wrestling with the same problem in her experiments with replacement skin. The two struck it off and agreed to work together to look for ways of speeding up the treatment. Although they did not yet realise it, they had crossed the threshold into entrepreneurship – they had moved from problem seeking to problem solving

Entrepreneurs solve the problems of others. Simply put like this, everybody can become one. However, to succeed, entrepreneurs need a battery of skills, a strong motivation and much more.

In many cases, I've discovered successful entrepreneurs have been shaped by some bad experience in childhood that affected them or their family. For someone like Fiona, who had supportive parents and a happy childhood, that doesn't seem to apply. Yet there was one trauma in her early years which may have cast a shadow over the household – the shattering of her father's dreams of becoming a professional footballer.

When she was a child, her father signed to play for Nottingham Forest, then one of the best teams in England. Had it gone well his life would have been transformed. Instead, he suffered a badly broken leg, bad enough to end his career there and then. It was a bitter blow when he had to return to working underground in the coalmine near Frickley. Could her father's disappointment have provided something of an extra motivation in Fiona's case? Certainly, a strong motivation and success as an entrepreneur go very much together.

However, without Marie Stone, the path to the breakthrough may have been much more tortuous than it was to prove. Marie was a medical scientist with a laboratory where the two women could work together to find a better way to grow and transfer the artificial skin that could save the lives of burns victims. Striking up a partnership with Marie showed Fiona possessed another entrepreneurial talent, the ability to gather up resources on the cheap.

They began to work together in 1993 and initially concentrated on improving the process of growing skin and transplanting it, employing the American technique of cultivating and harvesting new skin. As we've seen, it meant taking a small piece of outer skin from an undamaged part of a burns patient and growing it into a sheet of skin that the body would see as 'self', genetically the same as the patient's own skin.

While it resolved the problem of rejection associated with donor skin (when the grafted skin is perceived by the body as foreign and therefore rejected), it presented many problems. First, it took too long to grow the new skin, typically 21 long days during which the patient was at risk of a deadly infection. Meanwhile, getting the new skin to take remained a major headache, since it was delicate and given to tearing.

Fiona found it all frustrating: "It takes a long time, it's fragile, it's difficult to use and after a while Marie and I thought, 'Well, we've got to be able to think about how to do this better.'"

Then she had a flash of inspiration: "What if we took some healthy skin from a patient with burns, chopped it up into very small pieces, then added some enzymes to break it down into a liquid. We could then try spraying this 'liquid skin' on to the patient's badly burned areas."

Given the growth of scientific knowledge about how the skin works and advances in the understanding of skin anatomy, Marie thought this was an approach worth trying. The two women had soon produced a form of liquid skin that could be sprayed directly onto the damaged region. The initial trials, conducted in great secrecy at Royal Perth, showed promising results. Using liquid skin had the advantage of creating a form of skin that grew faster, taking only five days for the liquid to grow in volume to cover a full square metre. This time saving was crucial in the battle to beat infection. The women then began a search to find the best available sprays, deciding on one that emitted a very fine jet of liquid skin.

Only after these secret trials were completed did the pair launch themselves into business. First, they took out a patent to protect their intellectual property. The business was launched in 1999 under the name Clinical Cell Culture (or 3Cs). It was to be a not-for-profit organisation,

with any surplus funds channelled into a trust set up by Fiona – the Harold McComb Foundation – in honour of her mentor at the hospital.

At this stage, Fiona and Marie had not realised quite what was involved in running a new 'tech' business. They were content to grow the business slowly by word of mouth recommendation. All this had to change in the wake of the Bali bombings. The media reported that the quite astonishing survival rates of victims were due to the new spray-on skin. It became a talking point on the radio and TV, and in the press.

It seemed a good time to begin a potentially global business in Fiona's view. As we have learnt, she was dedicated to ridding the world of unnecessary pain. Burns victims are among the worst sufferers, since the pain of deep burns could last for months. She and Marie had already found that the new spray could cure burns more quickly and reduce scarring. It also clearly reduced pain.

The obstacle that lay in the way of achieving her long-term goals was the up-front costs of starting a tech business. For starters, there was the expense of registering the patents, which had to be renewed and increased as the scientific side of the business came up with improvements.

Medicine is particularly capital intensive in that the business is highly regulated, with the regulations varying across continents and trading areas. Given the cut-throat competition, there's a constant need to advertise and market the products. All these factors push up the cost of launching a company, and force entrepreneurs to turn to stock markets, venture capitalists or both. The result is that the entrepreneurs who started the company may find themselves outnumbered on the board, and forced to accept changes in both policy and personnel.

The first hiccup came when the 3Cs company took steps to bring experience and business know-how onto the board. At the heart of the company's strategy was the need to win the American regulator's approval for the new spray-on technology and its ability to speed recovery.

Dealing with the US Food and Drug Administration (FDA) is a notoriously tricky job and the 3Cs company found itself in difficulties over a technical point. News that the FDA was dragging its feet on this

issue had an impact on the company share price and led to a shake-up. The company name was changed to Avita Medical, new people were brought onto the board and the emphasis within the company shifted to address the potential worldwide market for cosmetic treatments.

It was seen as a knock back for the project but entrepreneurs must be ready for such a thing. Persistence in pursuit of the greater vision is one of the cardinal virtues of the entrepreneur. In May 2009, such determination was rewarded when it was announced that the US Air Force Institute of Regenerative Medicine was to invest US$47 million to fast track the approval of Spray-on, now renamed ReCell®, as a regenerative and reconstructive treatment for badly burnt servicemen.

This boost – lifting the share price by twenty-five per cent – was followed by further progress in 2012 when the FDA announced ReCell® could be put through the necessary trials to prove its safety and effectiveness. This meant that by the end of 2012 the new treatment would have started on its journey to full approval for civilian use

Although the company had yet to make a profit, it was well on the way to breaking even. Fiona, as a director, was paid some $200,000 AS dollars in the latest financial year, with most of this money going directly to the McComb Foundation to fund further research.

Fiona's business is committed to leading the field in tissue engineering technology for skin. Product development has continued since the establishment of the proprietary culturing techniques, which has resulted in the commercial availability of several innovative products to improve the quality of life for many patients around the world. The existing product range is supported by sound research and development that will result in the release of new technologies to provide real and needed solutions in the clinical and laboratory arenas.

What about the challenges of commercialising the research?

"That sort of commercialisation is probably, in retrospect, the hardest thing I've ever been involved in because I have no education or training in that regard," said Fiona.

Is there anything that can prepare you for it?

"I'm not sure. It's interesting: I speak now at innovation sessions and things like that for the university, and speak to the commercial science side, and I say that you can't have one without the other, it's a symbiosis. If you expect your idea to be the best thing since sliced bread and expect everything from it, you'll be disappointed. Equally, if you expect to get everything out of others' ideas without rewarding the inventors appropriately you will be disappointed, because they won't support the commercialisation and they won't give you the next idea. I don't know whether that falls on deaf ears or whether people are listening."

So Fiona found a problem, solved it and then turned the solution into a successful business. This, as we have seen in this book, is the core of entrepreneurial success: find a problem, solve it and sell the solution widely. However, in Fiona's case, her motive was not to make money for personal gain. Her driver was to raise funds to plough back into the McComb Foundation, enabling it to continue its groundbreaking research.

Thus, it has been something of a rollercoaster ride, but with the way ahead looking smoother does Fiona regret becoming one of Australia's few 'tech' entrepreneurs? She doesn't think of it that way. Her department has grown in both size and authority, while the story of Spray-on skin has given others ideas of starting up wealth-producing businesses and creating the jobs that come with them. She remains as keen as ever to promote the case for getting out there and discovering new ways to improve human health and comfort.

In recent interviews with students at Coolbinia Primary School, Fiona was asked:

Q. Did you ever feel that your plans had failed, and at which point?
"I think plans failing is a really interesting question. I've been on a long journey. I'm 54 now and that's seriously old. I hope I still have heaps of years to go. Every day there's new success and some failures. But believe you me you can always get better – but things don't always go how you'd expect all the time. What you have to do is pick yourself up and keep going. That's part of life."

Q. Have you ever not wanted to go to work?

"I had a situation way back when I first started, when I didn't have such a strong team, when I thought that maybe I just wasn't good enough. It was very early when I had been doing the job for not very long, about a year, and I thought I should be able to do better but I realised that the only way to do better was to go back and work at it. So I went back to work and I have been there ever since."

Here we see two key entrepreneurial traits – persistence and recovery from setbacks – which we have encountered many times in this book.

What is Fiona's philosophy on life? "If you are happy in what you do you will be productive and probably successful. If you get up in the morning really looking forward to your day then achievement will follow from this."

So find something that you feel passionate about and stick with it.

Fiona's story is an inspiring one, which clearly demonstrates many of the attributes required by successful entrepreneurs, although I doubt whether Fiona would class herself as an entrepreneur! It's a story of serving an apprenticeship, hard work, finding a passion, solving problems and committing to a lifelong cause. In doing so, Fiona worked out what her lifelong purpose was and she should be proud of her achievements and the legacy she will leave behind.

As a one-time athlete of some promise, let us end by giving Fiona the last word:

"We've got to raise the bar. We've got to bring our medical students into the understanding that they can actually go out there and find out things that are new, that are novel, that can change people's lives in an innovative way...Get to it."

Lessons Learned

- Find something you are really passionate about and this can become your life's work.
- Find a problem, solve it and sell the solution as widely as possible.
- Stay persistent when the going gets tough.
- Find a worthwhile partner who shares your passion, vision and complements your skills.
- Entrepreneurship is not always about making money for yourself. It can be about creating something of real value from practically nothing.

Chapter Fifteen

entrecode® – Unlocking the Entrepreneurial DNA

I have tried to tell the story in this book of my journey to crack the entrepreneurial code over a 20-year period.

In this chapter I summarise the actual research findings of our study of over 300 entrepreneurs in the UK and Australia. The **entrecode**® factors were the ones which highly correlated with the entrepreneurs who were the most successful over a 10-year period.

If you have got this far in the book then this next chapter should hold no surprises for you.

The entrepreneurs in this book are people who live and breathe the **entrecode**® factors every day of their lives.

If you have been inspired enough to want to follow in the footsteps of successful entrepreneurs then I have outlined the **entrecode**® in this chapter in more detail. I also set out how entrepreneurs use the code in their day-to-day work. You can practise the steps in the code in order to develop your business and your chances of success. If you are really up for it you will find your own way of undertaking some of the steps.

I wish you the very best in using the **entrecode**® to boost your business.

Good luck!

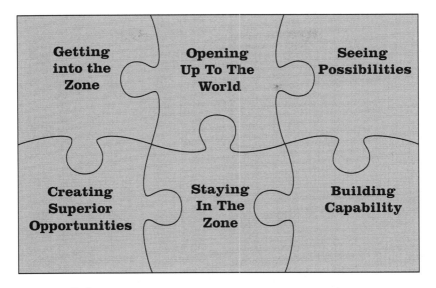

entrecode®

Getting Into The Zone	
The entrepreneurial mindset that creates success	
Factor	Description
Achievement Drive	Acts with determination and purpose to achieve results.
Compelling Vision	A picture of what the end game will look like which is highly motivating.
Goal Directed Energy	High levels of energy to make things happen.
Action Oriented	Takes the initiative and takes actions quickly.

Opening Up To The World	
Connecting with the world	
Factor	Description
Expressing Passion	Expresses ideas in a highly persuasive and inspiring manner.
Purposeful Networking	Builds and maintains networks of useful business relationships.
Creates Partnerships	Negotiating deals and builds strong commercial partnerships.

Seeing Possibilities Joining the dots	
Factor	**Description**
Big Picture	Focuses on the strategic big picture.
Options Thinking	Creates a wide range of alternatives to resolve issues.
Savvy	Relies on intuition and experience to guide judgments.

Creating Superior Opportunities Opportunities which are highly profitable with a sustainable competitive advantage	
Factor	**Description**
Problem Seeking	Seeks to find where customers have a problem the need resolving.
Synthesis	Integrates new information in order to develop new approaches.
Problem Solving	Creates solutions to customers' problems that create new business opportunities.
Delighting Customers	Ensures that the customer's experiences are exceptional.

Staying In The Zone Use it or lose it	
Factor	**Description**
Focus	Stays focused on priorities, avoiding distractions.
Positive Mindset	Stays positive through all circumstances.
Self-Determining	Comfortable making own decisions which will shape own destiny.
Persistence	Persistent at seeing things through and recovering well from setbacks.

Building Capability Building the business capacity to grow	
Factor	Description
Building the Team	Building a strong team by selecting and motivating the right people.
Ensuring systems and processes are installed	Creating the culture, systems and processes that serve the business.
Experiential Learning	Learns by doing and from successful peers.

Cracking the entrepreneurial code was a bit like putting a jigsaw together, piece by piece in order to see the full picture. Now let's look at the pieces of the jigsaw in more detail.

The Entrepreneurial Zone

The entrepreneurs in our research operate in what we have termed 'The Entrepreneurial Zone'. This is similar to the notion used by top athletes of getting into 'the zone' by which they mean getting their mind and bodies focused and coordinated. This fusion of mind and body enables them to achieve success.

The same is true for successful entrepreneurs. They have an extremely focused way of thinking and behaving which creates the drive and energy required to succeed.

"When I get into my zone I can fly! I write down the first two sentences before I begin (presentations, meetings, negotiations) then I go on intuition. This gets me into the zone and then I am unstoppable"

Catherine Speed, UPCO.

The key components of the entrepreneurial zone are:

- Drive and the need to achieve success
- Compelling vision
- Goal-directed energy

- Proactive action oriented
- Persistence

Let's take each in turn.

Drive and the need to achieve success

Drive is a key entrepreneurial process. It provides the energy to create a valued business and to keep going through adversity and setbacks.

Drive is associated with questions about IDENTITY. Who am I? and Why am I here? It is also about DESTINY. What am I meant to do? This might sound strange but it is the source of most entrepreneurs' energy and passion.

"A drive is an innate disposition towards the implementation of own goals. Drives are factors motivating human behaviour. Primary drives have a physiological basis whereas acquired drives have been learned through life experience. Acquired drives are often triggered by the environment and sparked by a life-changing event." Sorry that's Wyatt speak, here is how I described drive:

"A drive is an internal energising force which is under control, whereas an obsession is an uncontrolled force."

An achievement drive is the tendency to work with determination towards a specific end that is considered important by the individual. Successful entrepreneurs have a very high need to achieve success. This stems from early life experiences of both a positive and negative nature.

Negative (examples)

- Failing exams at school and feeling they let themselves and others down.
- An overwhelming negative experience – got to get away from this.
- Being bullied at school.
- Family marriage break up.
- Being told at school "you will never achieve anything".
- A failure to achieve childhood dreams, i.e., to make the first eleven at sport.

- Unsure what job to take and having several false starts.
- Being embarrassed by poor handwriting or even dyslexia.
- Sibling rivalry, particularly the middle child.

Positive (examples)
- Finding a friend (mentor) who really believed in them and encouraged them.
- Having their real talents revealed to them, for example by vocational guidance.
- Making something really difficult happen – which made them proud.
- Discovering they had qualities that they never imagined they had.

The negative experiences lead to the creation of a very strong drive:

> "I will prove to myself and others that I am OK"
> Simon Woodroffe, Yo Shushi

> "I will do whatever it takes to achieve success"
> Wayne Rowlett, Kwok Foods

John Cauldwell of Phones4U recalls his drive coming from seeing the dejected look on his parents face when he failed his eleven plus. This rang bells with me. This is about moving away from failure or disappointment.

The positive experiences lead to the recognition of what entrepreneurs want from life and that it might be possible to achieve. This dream or aspiration is very positive and is strongly held by successful entrepreneurs. This is about **moving towards success**.

> "This combination, of moving away from failure and/or towards achieving a dream, provides the energy and rocket fuel in successful entrepreneurs. It also reminds us that success often comes out of adversity (earning it) as opposed to privilege (deserving it). Our research suggests that without this strong drive and need for achievement; entrepreneurs are unable to maintain the energy and commitment necessary to create a successful high growth business."
> Wyatt Woodsmall

Wyatt and Marilyne Woodsmall suggest that "Perhaps 10–15% of the population has this drive. Our work with American athletes suggests that perhaps a further 10% of the population may have the potential for this drive and that it may be possible to reveal it and nurture it." A key test, therefore, at start up for potential entrepreneurs is to establish if they have the drive already, or if it is latent, and then whether it can be encouraged and developed.

The issue with latent entrepreneurs is to reveal to them, via the Entrepreneurial Potential Report, that they have entrepreneurial talents. This in itself may be sufficient to create the drive. Others may be more problematic. They may require a level of coaching to encourage individuals to recognise their entrepreneurial potential and act upon it.

Compelling Vision

The purpose of the vision is to provide focus and direction for everybody concerned with the enterprise. It enables people to determine their priorities, i.e. "What should we be doing right now?" Entrepreneurs by nature are turned on by new things or projects. These can be distractions that take the focus off the key priorities. A clear vision provides a discipline which entrepreneurs need if they are going to achieve their aims. A clear vision also acts as a motivator when the going gets tough. Keep going, because the prize is worth it.

Finally, it helps entrepreneurs to sell their business story to others including customers, suppliers, staff and investors.

Enthusiasm and passion are alluring and attract positive interest and energy. Entrepreneurs develop a magnetism which attracts people to them. Here's how they do it.

Imagine a superior opportunity 5 or 10 years into the future. What will success look like? If it was 2020 and the entrepreneur was reflecting on their business life, what would need to have happened for them to feel delighted with what they had achieved? For example would their products/service be a leader in the region, the UK, Europe or the World? How large would the enterprise be? What role would they ideally have played? Would they feel that they have discovered who they are and have

they proven to themselves and others that they are OK? Would their family and friends be really proud of them?

In describing the vision they try to create a cause worth fighting for. For example, one biotech company honestly believes that they are engaged in finding a cure for breast cancer. People can buy into this noble purpose. At the opposite end, one entrepreneur said his vision was to become a millionaire. His team found it a little difficult to get excited by his self-interested personal goal.

Entrepreneurs are careful about grand statements that are just empty words and that fool no one. For example 80 percent of UK manufacturing businesses claim to be 'world class', yet only 2 percent come anywhere near measurable world class criteria.

Successful entrepreneurs also envision the way of getting to their ultimate goal. They imagine the journey as well as the destination. Often they start with the end game in mind and work backwards to the present.

The first stage in the process of visioning is to imagine what success will look like.

Some entrepreneurs create a film or video of the future in their mind, and they see themselves being successful. They then replay the video whenever the going gets tough in order to remind them of the prize.

> "I have a video of the future; I find it really helpful in
> staying focused and motivated."
> *Tony Burpee, Applied Cytometry Supplies.*

The vision needs to be compelling and exciting, and it should fire people up and should inspire them when they think about it. The more colourful the picture is the better. If they can't imagine it, they cannot bring it to life.

The second stage is that the vision needs to be focused. Not "we are going to be a big player in the construction industry" but "we will be the leader in community regeneration in the North of England", which was Keepmoat's vision.

Success comes from focus and not from scattered effort. Once the vision is established the entrepreneur needs to commit to it 110 percent.

In selecting the vision the entrepreneur must by definition sacrifice other opportunities. Learning to say "no" as well as "yes" is a key discipline for entrepreneurs. Too many opportunities are the enemy of focus and commitment – they simply distract people and take energy away from the delivery of the vision.

Finally, entrepreneurs need to expect their vision to manifest. This is not arrogance or naiveté, but it's simply a genuine conviction that it will happen. This is beyond hope, belief or desperation. It's the locus of control. This is going to happen. It's no big deal. Once they expect it, their behaviour and actions start to become congruent with the vision. They start behaving as if it's about to happen.

This is the psychological ownership which is critical to success. Winners look like they expect to win, not come in second. You can see it in their eyes and their demeanor, and people can sense it.

You need to expect your vision to be achieved. Otherwise you may well fail by inadvertently communicating your self-doubts to others, who are critical to your success.

> "Every day I do not spend working towards my vision is a
> day wasted."
>
> *Wayne Rowlatt, Kwok Foods.*

Successful entrepreneurs translate their vision into a framework. This is like a book. The overall goal is the title, with the key milestones being the chapter headings. Within each chapter are the details. The entrepreneur can see the title, book or chapters or get down into specific detail on a page. The important point is that the entrepreneur is able to see the overall picture and how the pieces fit together. This is similar to a critical path flowchart.

Goal Directed Energy

Entrepreneurship is a high energy process, and anything which deflects or dilutes this energy adds cost, not value, to the process. A useful analogy

is to think of goal directed energy as a laser beam locked onto a specific target. This is the opposite of the shotgun approach of trying anything and desperately hoping that it might work.

Goal directed energy had the highest correlation with entrepreneurial success with over 300 successful entrepreneurs worldwide in our cracking the code research. It is the key process that links vision and dreams to results.

Here is how successful entrepreneurs do it.

First, they have a very clear vision to start from. When faced with options on how to spend their time or resources, they ask: "Given the vision what is the priority right now?" This enables them to stay focused on the strategic priority. One entrepreneur described the process as 'keeping your eyes on the prize'.

The next question they ask is "what is the next step to move that priority forward?" This is the sequencing question. A journey of a thousand miles starts with a single step. The crucial question is what is the first step? Or as Hugh Facey of Gripple said: "First things first and second things not at all."

Finally they delete everything else. This is the equivalent of pressing the delete button on the computer. In successful entrepreneurs this process of 'prioritise, sequence, delete' becomes a natural way of operating. They do it unconsciously and avoid the 'busy fool' syndrome and the tendency to confuse activity with productivity.

This process also enables entrepreneurs to stay persistent. Distractions are the enemy of progress. Entrepreneurs know to avoid anything which distracts them from the achievement of their goal.

Those entrepreneurs who don't already have the 'prioritise sequence delete' program imprinted in their unconscious mind can be helped by providing processes like the prioritising tools in my book 'Doing the Business'. Toolkit 6 in this book sets out a number of practical ways that entrepreneurs can prioritise their activities.

In reality the really successful entrepreneurs don't engage in any activity which is not goal directed. Everything that they do has a clear purpose

which is the delivery of the vision. For example, they don't network unless it's with people who can directly help them. Clear vision and goal directed energy are important keys in the journey to success.

Proactive Action Oriented

"Just do it!" is the successful entrepreneur's mantra. There are a number of explanations for the entrepreneurs' drive to get on with things and therefore the frustration they often feel when having to deal with people and systems that are slow and bureaucratic. Entrepreneurs have a real need for immediacy. What makes them action oriented? It is primarily their drive and their personality type. Successful entrepreneurs are normally the 'get on with it' type. So when trying to work with entrepreneurs you ignore their action orientation at your peril. If you appear slow or bureaucratic, they will simply avoid you! However, there is a downside to their style, which is that they don't reflect much in their experiences, so they can repeat the same mistakes. So getting them to reflect can be a very helpful intervention.

Secondly, they get bored with detail. So they may not spend enough time focused on developing high quality solutions, they prefer a quick fix. This can reduce the quality of their business opportunity. So helping them put a team together of people who complement their style and cover their weaknesses can also be very helpful.

Opening Up to the World

Expressing Passion

Many of the entrepreneurs in our research were not raging extroverts as perhaps the stereotype suggests. Often quiet and sometimes introverted, preferring to just get on and do things… Until you ask them about their business and then watch them come alive! Their eyes light up and they become animated, talking with passion in a highly persuasive and infectious manner. This metamorphose is very useful in persuading customers to buy, banks to lend and employees to go that extra mile. It is the source of the energy and commitment seen generally only in small entrepreneurial, sometimes family firms. It's the petrol in the tank that drives the engine. It's also what makes entrepreneurs interesting people.

Purposeful Networking

Purposeful networking starts with having clear business goals. Then they start to notice things which can help them to achieve their goals. The poet Goethe said "Once you have a clear goal the world conspires to help you." The analogy is similar to making a decision to purchase a new car. Until the decision is made you hardly notice the make of your chosen car on the road. Once the decision is made to purchase a new car you start seeing your car – in adverts, on the TV, on the street and virtually everywhere. The vision brings a new significance to information which entrepreneurs suddenly start noticing, and which they then synthesise into helping them to achieve their vision. This is a natural process which engages both the conscious and unconscious mind. It's as if entrepreneurs connect to the world in a new way which helps them to gather information, which will help them achieve their goals.

> "Once I am clear where I am going I start to trip over things
> which can help me. It's a weird process but it works."
> *Wayne Rowlatt, Kwok Foods.*

A second process entrepreneurs use to network is building a neural network. This is a network of individuals that they have learned to trust and value. This 'selective entourage' can be friends, colleagues, customers – in fact anybody whose opinions and wisdom the entrepreneur values. Wisdom comes from multiple perspectives.

The neural network is a bit like creating a super computer of linked minds, which the entrepreneur uses to test out ideas, problems, strategies or concerns, in fact any issue which they want to check out. They use this network to check, cross check and get different perspectives. It's a bit like a virtual board that they can call on at any time.

> "I have people who operate like a virtual board, I couldn't
> afford to pay them but they provide invaluable support,
> particularly when the going gets tough. We talk things
> through and it really helps."
> *Catherine Speed, UPCO.*

The third process is targeted networking with a purpose. All successful entrepreneurial activity is goal directed. Entrepreneurs don't network for networking sake. They identify what they need, identify who can help and then actively try to build a relationship with that person in order to help them to build a valued business.

The Chinese have a word for targeted networking – Guanxi. A highly successful Chinese entrepreneur described the process as follows: "We make contact with people we think can help us. We turn these contacts into friendships. From there we get contracts. We turn the contracts into alliances and then into partnerships. If all goes well the next stage is that we become family!"

This stage is about building and using networks with people who can help build the business. Successful entrepreneurs dedicate between 30 to 50 percent of their time to this vital process.

Creating Partnerships

Successful entrepreneurs are deal makers. In order to secure deals they build strong commercial partnerships. Few businesses have all the resources, know how or know who so they need to partner with other people or organisations that can help them. It's the synergy principle of $1 + 1 = 3$.

Seeing Possibilities

Big Picture

Entrepreneurs are generally good at seeing the big picture. They can see what customers need, where the industry is heading, what the competition are doing and therefore where the opportunities exist. They are strategic in their thinking. However, many get bored with the detail and have a low boredom threshold. So they need people around them who can do the detail and sweep up after them. In my own case I have brilliant P.A. who makes sure I don't miss the detail and mess things up!

Options Thinking

Entrepreneurs are usually very good at creating options to solve problems. Plan A fails, straight into Plan B, then Plan C until they resolve the issue.

Their problem solving approach is:

1. I have done this before (experiences) I will just do it again;

2. 'Phone a friend' call someone in their network (hence the importance of networking) who might be able to help;

3. Call someone who might know someone or

4. Just try something and we will get success or learning.

It seems that about 20 percent of the general population are options thinkers, the rest are procedural thinkers. If a procedural thinker gets stuck they usually need an options thinker to give them a new option.

Savvy
Savvy is streetwise judgment which comes from experiences or intuition. Entrepreneurs usually believe in following their gut feeling. When they are proven right this reinforces their self-belief. If it goes wrong then they are back into options thinking to create a new solution. There is a difference between savvy and arrogance. One is based upon experience and genuine intuition, the other on inflated ego.

Savvy is also the commercial ability to see where the money can be made in any deal. High performing people are commercially smart and savvy.

Creating Superior Opportunities
Creating superior opportunities is at the heart of the **entrecode**®. It is the way entrepreneurs create opportunities to build great businesses. Entrepreneurs create superior opportunities by:

- Finding a customer problem
- Solving it
- Then selling the solution to others

A superior opportunity is one that has:

- Major market growth potential
- A high gross margin
- A defensible competitive advantage
- Is new, different and interesting

- Solves a real customer's problems
- Creates new potential opportunities
- Attracts media attention and creates a lot of interest

Many start up opportunities are 'me-too' products and services. They are no different from what already exists; hence they are hard to sell and often have to compete on price alone. Consequently they find it hard to attract willing investors.

So how do entrepreneurs create superior opportunities?
Entrepreneurs help customers to articulate the problems they have – even when they are unaware of them. Then they set out to resolve them and in doing so they create a new product or service. This ensures that they develop opportunities which customers actually want as opposed to ideas which only they themselves are interested in.

- Salim Zilka's wife complained that she had to visit several shops in order to purchase the goods she needed for her young children. Zilka at that time owned 12 chemist shops. So he combined his chemist shop with a clothes shop, a pram shop and a toyshop and called it 'Mothercare' – the one stop shop to make it easy for mothers to shop for their children.

- Tony Burpee deliberately sought his customers' problems. "I asked them what was keeping them awake at night. I then offered to fix their problems. They loved it and this was usually the start of a long term relationship."

- The customers of Hugh Facey, who sold wire, complained that when their wire fences broke they ripped their fingers mending them. So Facey developed a simple device which rejoined broken fences, and the Gripple was born. This made it easy for customers to repair fences.

It is worth repeating that during the course of undertaking this research we found an amazing statistic in Timmons book *New Venture Creation*. Read it slowly and think of the implications for supporting entrepreneurs:

Ninety-five percent of all the radical innovations in products and services during the last century were from small firms of less than 20 people who listened to their customers and set out to resolve their problems.

Entrepreneurs also use a number of algorithms often unconsciously to create new business opportunities:

Do the Opposite

Catherine Speed of UPCO asked the large corporate clients what they disliked about IT software and training suppliers. She then turned these dislikes into her benefits and has built a multimillion pound business as a result.

Become the Customer

Hanson Brick salesmen worked in one of their customers' businesses for a period trying to sell their own products. They identified 11 problems that they were inadvertently giving their customers. They quickly sorted these out and became the preferred supplier.

Fusion

Derwent Valley Foods created a brand new concept in adult snack food by fusing together some key elements:

- Crisps were for children not adults.
- More people were travelling abroad and experiencing continental foods.
- Dinner parties and in- home entertainment were in a growth phase.

They fused these ideas together to create snack foods for adults from around the world. They called the brand 'Phileas Fogg'. This enabled them to quadruple the price of crisps. This is the benefit of a superior opportunity.

So far we have discovered 20 algorithms to create new business opportunities. A potential added value intervention would be to provide entrepreneurs with the algorithms to encourage them to turn a 'me-too' offer into a superior opportunity.

Once they notice something interesting, entrepreneurs set up low cost experiments or pilots to test out their ideas in practice. They use these pilots to shape up their opportunities. They get success or learning from the pilots.

In order to create superior opportunities entrepreneurs normally have to push the boundaries of what exists. They need to 'raise the bar', set 'impossible' new standards and be assertive with people in order to get them to strive and be persistent in reaching the dream.

Wayne Rowlatt when he worked for Kwok Foods (who made Chinese food for two major retailers) puts this very clearly: "When I ask my production team to try something new and they complain that "it will be really difficult for us", then I know my customers will usually love it and my competitors often won't be bothered to copy us." This is the basis of a superior opportunity.

Successful entrepreneurs talk about getting into the heads of their customers and really try to understand their business. Catherine Speed (UPCO) describes her task as "trying to understand my customers' business better than they do."

Many successful entrepreneurs spend 30 percent or more of their time with their customers gathering intelligence. A key test of whether entrepreneurs are actually on the right track in developing a superior opportunity is how much time customers are prepared to spend with them.

Staying in the Zone

Focus
Entrepreneurs maintain focus by being clear about priorities and prioritising their time. They 'lock-on' to the things they need to do to make their business a success. They recognise you cannot have 37 priorities by definition.

Positive Mindset
The entrepreneurs in our study generally had a positive mindset. They expected to succeed and mostly saw the cup half full not empty. They believed they could learn, grow and develop. This is the opposite of a

doom and gloom fixed mindset 'the world is a terrible place, we are doomed and there is nothing I can do about it'. Accept your lot. You are what you are…

Successful entrepreneurs have a positive mindset very similar to top athletes. This enables them to stay persistent through adversity and to create something new and distinctive – to 'go where no one has been before'. Successful entrepreneurs create a new unique opportunity and inspire and enthuse others by their persistent upbeat approach. Their positive mindset is there in their normal state, but also they can retain it during a crisis.

Their strategies for maintaining a positive mindset include:

- Having a positive picture in their mind of them succeeding, i.e. a compelling vision. Hugh Facey of Gripple developed a novel device for mending wire fences and described his vision as: "the smile on the face of farmers when they use my device and don't rip their hands to shreds and they tell me this is a fantastic product. They love it!"

- An internal voice which says "I feel good". The tonality of the voice is important as well as the content. The tonality is upbeat and positive.

When entrepreneurs hit a crisis they create a picture of what's needed to fix it. They then set out to use the picture to guide their behaviour and to stay positive.

Self Determining

The entrepreneurs were very self-confident and happy to determine and decide their own future. They do not need external verification that they are on the right track. They just seem to be able to make a decision and live with any uncertainty. Some of this comes from past experiences where they have been successful, they know what to do. It also comes from their self-confident personality type.

BUILDING CAPABILITY

Entrepreneurs consciously develop the capability of their business in their quest to build a valued business.

Unless entrepreneurs build the capability in their business, they are always playing catch up in terms of systems, people, and processes. And this can cause major problems.

Entrepreneurs recognise the need to work on as well as in the business. This means spending time building the capability of the business as well as spending time running the day to day business.

Entrepreneurs focus on three key areas in building the capability of their business.

Building a team

Successful entrepreneurs understand their own strengths and weaknesses. They build a team by recruiting people with the same values but complimentary skills. They recognise they cannot be good at everything so they try to get the best people by possibly can to ensure the team is balanced. Their aim is $1+1+1 = 10$, the synergy that comes from the team working really effectively together.

Ensuring systems and processes are installed

In order to get consistency into their processes and procedures, entrepreneurs generally resist the pressure from traditional advisors to document everything, to create policies and to formulate detailed bureaucratic procedures.

They often establish controls by encouraging people to take personal responsibility for making things happen efficiently and effectively. They trust people, and the majority of their people respond positively.

Where processes are required they prefer one page bullet point guidelines of 'our way of doing business'. They work hard at not allowing the achievement culture to become a power-driven bureaucracy. This is important, because the advice they normally get from the establishment is to plan, formalise and systemise things.

They build their culture by recruiting people who share their values. They also walk the talk. "My rules for me and my rules for you" as Tony Burpee of Applied Cytometry Systems described it.

Typical values in use, as opposed to theory, shared by successful entrepreneurs include:

- Customer commitment
- Brutal honesty
- Treating people with integrity and respect
- Putting money back into the business
- Team working
- Humility
- Every person a business person
- Let's not take ourselves too seriously
- Do it now.

Successful entrepreneurs understand why the business works and establishes key indicators to take the process of their recipe for success on an on-going basis.

For example in Keepmoat's case the key indicators were:

- Delighting customers
- % of work won by negotiation (not tender)
- Gross margin %
- Work to progress (on time)
- Purchasing costs (supply chain)

Smart entrepreneurs invest ahead in the business rather than playing catch up. They will invest in the best IT systems that they can get in order to help them.

They also invest in their own development. "I was faced with a critical negotiation with a customer so I flew an expert in negotiating from Sweden over for one day to coach me. It cost 10k." said Hugh Facey of Gripple Ltd.

So in summary, building capability is a conscious on-going process of investing in working on as well as in the business. Smart entrepreneurs

invest ahead to enable the business to grow and to avoid having to play catch up.

Finally, they invest in their own development, so that they continue to be an asset as opposed to a liability to the business growth process.

Experiential Learning

At a very basic level, they learn from their experiences of doing business in order to avoid the 'repeat mistakes syndrome'. As mentioned earlier, entrepreneurs are doers and not reflectors, so they may need encouragement with this process.

In consciously reviewing past experiences and learning the lessons from their successes and mistakes, entrepreneurs build up their recipe for success.

They prefer to learn by personal problem solving, from successful peers, their team and their family.

This is why they often do not respond to the traditional systematic products of the support system. They reject training courses, business textbooks and advisors and consultants.

This explains why entrepreneurs enjoy talking to each other and sharing experiences. So putting them together in facilitated groups is highly valued by entrepreneurs. This provides opportunities for the support system to provide support in the ways entrepreneur's value.

Entrepreneurs develop the business by initiating low cost, low risk pilots. They try something, and if it works they build it into their business model. If it doesn't work, then they try something else. This trial and error do it again method is the action - oriented entrepreneurs preferred way of learning.

It is the opposite of the traditional business cycle of plan, do, review.

Chapter Sixteen
Conclusion and Vision

Twenty years ago Professor Allan Gibb challenged me to uncover how successful entrepreneurs started, grew and revitalised their businesses. This for me was the Holy Grail. If we could find it and de-code the secrets it contained, we would be doing humanity a priceless favour. For not even entrepreneurs fully understood what their craft consisted of.

Back in 1990 when the economies across the world were booming, motivating people to throw up their job to start up on their own did not seem to matter all that much. Nowadays, with unemployment rising around the world, it has become a matter of huge importance – only a blind fool would deny the imperative need to create new jobs, either by starting new businesses or shaking up existing ones.

Until now, there has always been an obstacle in the way, the lack of a book of instructions about just how to go about it.

Of course, there have been many books on entrepreneurship but mostly of the "copy-me" variety, as though all business were built using a standard blue-print. The outcome? A depressingly low creation of new businesses and existing businesses flat lining, there is no end in sight for people who have lost their jobs or have never had one.

This book set out to meet the problem head on. Since I started working with entrepreneurs in the 1980s I slowly came to realise that the biggest obstacle that faced many start-up companies is a failure to grasp the special nature of the entrepreneurial brain. Seeking help from other successful entrepreneurs could only go so far since entrepreneurs

themselves could not explain what made them choose one route rather than another. There was a barrier between what might be termed 'normal thinking' and 'entrepreneurial thinking'.

To maximise our chances of building a successful new business – or to revive an old one – we had to work out how to remove the barriers and crack the entrepreneurial code.

After years of effort I have finally done it, providing a guide and practical handbook that offers its secrets to anyone willing to spend time and patience re-inventing themselves as 'entrepreneurs'.

But have I really cracked the code?

Well don't take my word for it, if I have done my job well, having read the entrepreneurs' stories you should now be able to figure it out for yourself.

The **entre**code® had enabled entrepreneurs, who up until that point had been unconsciously competent to become consciously competent. They now understood how they became successful.

When I started out on this journey I didn't realise that people have been looking in the wrong place to uncover the entrepreneurs' recipe for success. The real breakthrough was provided by the insight that came from Wyatt Woodsmall's work in America with high performing sports people. It turned out that his remarkable techniques could be applied to aspiring entrepreneurs with dramatic effect.

Entrepreneurship, it turned out, was much more of a personal process than a business one. Having a compelling vision, recovering from setbacks and being persistent is far more important than budgets and plans in the world of entrepreneurs. This knowledge has become the foundation for the **entre**code®, a guide to how entrepreneurs create success. Having read the book you will have discovered how entrepreneurs used the **entre**code® to start, grow and revitalise their businesses. I invite you to follow in their footsteps.

As for my vision for the **entre**code®, I hope that schools and colleges will adopt it as the basis for their enterprise curriculum, sowing the seeds of an enterprise culture that could blossom sooner than seems possible.

Meanwhile we need to give a helping hand to those who dream of running their own business. A start can be made by reading this book, a preparation for taking that first step. Using the **problem seeking – problem solving** approach, get ready to go out there to spot that superior opportunity for yourself. The good news is that you don't need to be wealthy to find one – remember Ajaz Ahmed and Hugh Facey.

As for existing businesses that want to grow or revitalise themselves, you can take inspiration from Terry Bramall and Paul Mackie who have used the **entrecode**® to transform their businesses. Follow their lead and replicate their success. As we have seen, entrepreneurs do not only create wealth, they improve people's lives, as the Fiona Woods story clearly illustrates.

I would be delighted if policy makers, government advisors, academics, business advisors and consultants adopted the **entrecode**® to really help entrepreneurs worldwide. As Tim says in his foreword, we hope that this book goes some way to convincing readers from a professional management background that we need to be more like entrepreneurs, rather than deriding their management approach and encouraging them to be more like us!

There are pockets of great practice, people who really understand and promote the **entrecode**® process; Tim Atterton in Australia, Dinah Bennett and Professor Allan Gibb around the world, Gideon Maas in England and Jagadish Shenoy in India. The challenge now is to spread the word more widely.

Finally if countries use the **entrecode**® to create wealth and jobs by adopting friendly and supportive policies for entrepreneurs, maybe we would hear less about austerity and more about growth.

The **entrecode**® has been my passion and my life's work and I hope it's a legacy I can leave behind and be proud of its contribution.

Index

"David Hall has a real passion for understanding what works and how to make businesses work better. This book offers food for thought and practical advice as well as a fascinating insight into David's own approach to his craft."

Professor Ted Fuller, Lincoln Business School, University of Lincoln, UK

"The Entrecode bounces along like a holiday page-turner at the same time as delivering fresh insight drawn from fascinating individuals and their business achievements. Loved it."

Dr Simon Haslam, Entrepreneur and co-owner FMR Research

"David Hall has succeeded in making the discussion around entrepreneurship 'human'. Too often entrepreneurship publications only focus on technical issues neglecting the person behind everything – the entrepreneur. This book combines real life cases with sound advice on how entrepreneurs can improve themselves."

Dr Gideon Maas, Director,
Institute of Applied Entrepreneurship, Coventry University

"This book is a game changer for individuals, organisations and society at large."

Dinah Bennett, Director,
International Centre for Entrepreneurship and Enterprise

"David Hall's Entrecode approach has helped us to transform the fortunes of our business."

Charlie Spencer, Entrepreneur and Owner, The Spencer Group

This book is an impassioned plea for people with talent to roll up their sleeves and buckle down to the task of creating the new businesses that will offer new jobs and fresh hope to those badly hit by the current economic crisis. It argues that the pool of potential entrepreneurial talent is much larger than is commonly supposed.

After spending twenty years meeting entrepreneurs and seeing them at work, David Hall has at last broken through the ring of secrecy that surrounds the subject, an informal code of practice that has prevented most new businesses ever shaking themselves free of the curse of small firm inertia.

This book is the first fruit of a new research programme that aims to lift the small firms into a bigger league and boost job creation across the developed and developing world – and not before time.

Greg Dyke, Director General, BBC, 1994–2004

David Hall's book unlocks the DNA of ░░░░░░░░░░ over 20 years of know-how and shares ░ ░░░░░░░░░░░ of entrepreneurs. From the vision and c░░░░░░░░░░░ opportunity, to the persistence and determ░░░░ ░░░░░░░░░░░ the inevitable obstacles. Using extensive research and unique analysis, Entrecode identifies 21 key factors of entrepreneurship.

With relevant and engaging stories from real-life entrepreneurs, this is an insightful and practical guide for everyone who aims to become an entrepreneur. It takes techniques from high performing athletes and applies them to setting up and growing a successful business, with inspiring results.

Entrecode is an excellent tool to help create a new generation of entrepreneurs. As well as revealing the secrets of educating for entrepreneurship, it will add value to both the entrepreneur and the wider economy. This isn't just another book about enterprise, it's a radical unveiling of the key traits of business success and how anyone can use them.

The Earl of Erroll, Chairman,
All-Party Parliamentary Group for Entrepreneurship